BASIL McIVOR was born in County Fermana
Methodist College, Belfast, and at Queen'
graduated in law. A retired resident magis
parliament as a Unionist MP in 1969, go
community relations and subsequently minister of education. He is o
the chairman of the board of governors at Lagan College, Northern Ireland's
first integrated school.

Hope Deferred

Experiences of an Irish unionist

Basil McIvor

THE
BLACKSTAFF
PRESS

BELFAST

First published in 1998 by
The Blackstaff Press Limited
3 Galway Park, Dundonald, Belfast BT16 0AN, Northern Ireland

This book has received support from the Cultural Traditions Programme
of the Community Relations Council, which aims to encourage
acceptance and understanding of cultural diversity.
The views expressed do not necessarily reflect those of the
NI Community Relations Council.

Basil McIvor has asserted his right under the
Copyright, Designs and Patents Act 1988 to be identified as
the author of this work.

Typeset by Techniset Typesetters, Newton-le-Willows, Merseyside

Printed in Ireland by ColourBooks Limited

A CIP catalogue record for this book
is available from the British Library

ISBN 0-85640-620-1

to
Jill

Hope deferred maketh the heart sick:
but when the desire cometh it is a tree of life.
PROVERBS 13:12

CONTENTS

ACKNOWLEDGEMENTS

This personal account of my life could not have been written without the encouragement and support of those who helped me on my way.

Especially do I owe a great deal to my wife Jill for her ready understanding and endless patience when, not finding the going easy, my spirits were at a low point. She gave me invaluable assistance, reading the first draft script and jogging my memory when necessary – as did Jonathan, Timothy and Jane who, as well, offered me much helpful and constructive criticism.

Had not George Gair, former New Zealand High Commissioner in London, suggested it, I doubt if I would have embarked on writing these memoirs at all. I thank him for the encouragement he gave me to do so.

I am greatly indebted to Colette Murray who cheerfully undertook the major task of reducing to some sort of order a great quantity of chaotic handwritten A4 pages on a word processor, a labour she performed with singular equanimity and impressive accuracy.

There are many others whose memories have assisted me on detail, when I had problems with my own, amongst whom are: Brian Baird, Bert Crooks, Ernest Gilmour, Trevor Hanna, John Kennedy, Frank Millar and Bill Slinger. And also the former principals of Lagan College, Terence Flanagan and Brian Lambkin.

I must express my real gratitude to those at Blackstaff Press who have given me much valued advice throughout the production of this book.

BASIL McIVOR
JANUARY 1998

INTRODUCTION

IT WAS WITH 'LIBERAL' TENDENCIES that I made an unlikely appearance on the political stage. I was not a political animal. One sunny Saturday afternoon in the summer of 1966 I received a telephone call, out of the blue, inviting me to allow my name to go forward for nomination as the Unionist Party candidate for the North Armagh seat in the Stormont parliament. Since then and to this day I cannot remember having met or spoken to the caller; nor can I, for the life of me, imagine why I was approached or what party political qualifications I was supposed to possess that would be appropriate material for a Unionist MP at Stormont. In particular I was not a member of the Orange Order, membership of which had hitherto been a *sine qua non* for election to a Unionist seat at Stormont. It was flattering but bizarre.

I failed to gain the nomination, but three years later I stood as a Unionist candidate in the new constituency of Larkfield which included all of Catholic Andersonstown (and the new developments of Twinbrook and Poleglass) in west Belfast. To the Unionist establishment I was a rank outsider. In his autobiography Terence O'Neill, recalling his visit to Andersonstown during the 1969 election campaign, observed that I was 'decent, moderate, but unknown'. He could have added – for good measure – rather too compliant, amenable and not by nature suited to the rough and tumble of those tumultuous times. By nature shy, I was to have to force myself to behave in ways that did not come naturally in order to meet the challenge I had imposed upon myself. On any objective view there was nothing in my temperament to indicate that I would eventually become a minister both in the Stormont government and subsequently in the powersharing Executive. I won Larkfield with a majority of some six thousand votes.

As a practising barrister, with a growing family to support, it was not the time to be caught up in the frustrations and complexities of Northern Ireland politics, especially when the harmony of the Unionist Party – which had ruled the region continuously and solely for almost fifty years – was in terminal decline. I had been establishing a comfortable practice, with some prospects. Life at the Bar demanded intensity of purpose and tireless industry. Prudence and plain common sense suggested that I keep my head down. I had a capacity for hard work, but not consistently in the same direction. I had got bored and so allowed myself to be drawn into politics as a 'liberal', condemned to swim against the tide of mistrust of the Unionist establishment – mistrust on the part of both the minority in Northern Ireland and the international community.

Challenging the integrity and fairness of Unionist domination in Northern Ireland never promised to be much fun – and it wasn't. But as moth to candle I found myself attracted to doing just that, and thus being drawn into the impending conflagration. Played out briefly at the most turbulent period in Irish history, my short political career was to evaporate in the candescent fury of the Protestant community in the rebellion of the 1974 Ulster Workers' Council strike.

It was a time that witnessed the most dramatic movements of local populations, the mounting toll of violent deaths amongst my fellow countrymen and -women and untold suffering and misery. Books about the period, which continue to tumble from publishers' presses, canvass every conceivable point in the political spectrum, save one – that of the Ulster Protestant liberal unionists who responded to Terence O'Neill's call for radical political and social reforms at his 'crossroads election' of 1969: 'What sort of Ulster do you want?' he asked. Few responded positively and Northern Ireland paid the price.

In politics I invested much emotional energy, albeit over a relatively short period of time, arguing within the Unionist Party against single-party government, and warning that the Unionist ship of state was heading for the rocks. In the end we went down with that ship which, within three years, had foundered. Much play was made of the phrase 'Ulster at the crossroads'. At one time or another we had been advised to take this road or that; but what the Unionist Party was doing at the time was standing, not at a crossroads, but on a cliff, staring blankly down at the acres of graves being dug, poised to plunge over to a grisly and largely unmourned death.

I don't very much care if my critics detect in this the arrogance of 'I told you so'. It is true that had the Unionist political establishment reacted much more positively to genuine grievances raised by the civil rights movement, things might have taken a different course. We might have avoided the unpitying, unforgiving consequences and the lost opportunities of the past quarter-century and more.

Anne Dickson, Robin Bailie and I formed the core of the liberal camp returned at the 1969 Stormont election. We were to flit briefly across the political stage (Robin more briefly than me) in a short but critical act in Northern Ireland's history. Ian Paisley derided us as either the 'Babes in the Wood' or the 'Three Blind Mice'. We took it as at least a form of flattery that we were taken notice of – the worst humiliation is to be ignored. But we went almost as quickly as we came. History should have told us that there was no place for liberal thinkers in Unionist orthodoxy.

These memoirs have allowed me to purge a lingering bitterness fuelled by frustration and sometimes fear. On the positive side they reassure me that a dramatic, and what for many was seen as a foolhardy, change of course was in the end vindicated. That change opened up for me, someone possessed of a latent sense of social justice I put down to my Methodism, much more exciting and rewarding opportunities to serve the larger community than offered by life at the Bar, which I did not find wholly fulfilling. Life has turned out to be a rich patchwork of change.

My views remain that the few slender hopes of resolving the 'Ulster problem' have always depended on the political viability of a Protestant liberal stance. This is no mere tautology in the sense that a solution is possible only if enough are prepared to compromise. It is the key to interpreting the Northern Ireland crisis. By Ulster Protestant liberalism I mean an emphasis on Irishness, at the least some notion of a broader Ulster nation, which sees no contradiction between being Irish and not wanting the borders of the country changed. This liberalism is inextricably linked with a recognition of the Catholic minority's legitimate right to a role in government.

Waves of Ulster Protestant liberalism have always destabilised Northern Ireland because they have been counterproductive. Orange reaction has consistently overwhelmed progressive movements and deepened religious cleavages. This has been so because reforms have been seen to have involved fundamental threats to Northern Ireland's constitutional position (and thus to the Protestants' economic and political status). The unionists' monopoly of political power is for them the guarantor of the constitutional status quo. There is a strong element of Ulster Protestant nationalism, not confined to the right wing or 'hardline', that holds that this constitutional position is embedded in a distinct culture and history and in the advantages of a relatively advanced state of economic development. This in turn is allied to a Protestant ethic as reflected in a familiar comment, 'that's more Protestant-looking', meaning 'more workmanlike'.

Northern Ireland is culturally distinct from both Britain and the Republic. My upbringing implanted in me the tacit, but deep-rooted, belief that Northern Ireland's economic position as well as her cultural identity was far superior to that of the South. In every area, 'British was best'. But loyalty to the Crown has always been conditional for the

Ulster Protestant. Both historically and in the present crisis, Protestants 'under siege' (as they see it) have been prepared to relegate loyalty to the British Crown in order to defend their Ulster heritage and economic ascendancy over Catholics.

Today, with equal opportunities in employment and vast sums of money being poured into Catholic as well as Protestant areas of need, the economic gap has been substantially reduced. This has come as a genuine cultural shock to many in Protestant housing estates who feel that they are being less favourably considered than those in Catholic housing estates. They, as Protestants, bewildered by loss of status, have lost their own defining point of reference – economic superiority to the Catholic minority. At the same time, the booming so-called Celtic Tiger economy of the South has undermined Northern Protestants' assumptions of superiority to the Republic.

It is in the Protestant housing estates that panic ultimately led to the recruitment of the Young Turks, loyalist terrorist paramilitaries, loyal to Britain only in a technical sense. In the 1970s unionist insecurity, fuelled by political developments, reached a high point. The flames were fanned by threats from outside – from the United States, Dublin, and what was perceived as a weak British government. And as internal compromise with the Catholic population implied, or seemed to imply, an external threat to Northern Ireland's constitutional position, a liberal approach became difficult if not impossible to argue.

Economic prosperity, however, was always only part of the larger whole of the Ulster Protestant identity. And those that see the development of economic cooperation within the European Union between Northern Ireland and the Republic of Ireland as the basis for resolving political conflict, fail to recognise this fundamental fact. Socialism has never played, and in the foreseeable future never will play, a significant part in Northern Ireland's politics. Class politics is completely subservient to the calling of the religious tribes. If it wasn't, the problem would have been resolved long ago – indeed by definition it would not exist.

The Protestants who settled in the north of Ireland from the sixteenth century onwards became, over four hundred years, Ulster men and women. They were Irish not English, with a belief in the distinctiveness of their own cultural identity which they saw as dependent on the

British link. But, in a supreme (or grotesque) irony, when it came to the Home Rule crisis they would fight the British to remain British – and not for the first time the 'siege mentality' was evoked. To see the Ulster Protestants as a minority inside Ireland, rather than a majority inside Northern Ireland, is to better understand their motivations – especially at crisis points and after the demoralising effect of the past thirty years. It helps explain their reactions to the proposals for reforms made in the wake of the civil rights marches of the sixties, and it helps explain the strike that brought down the powersharing Executive.

The short-lived Ulster liberal revival ushered in by Terence O'Neill was rapidly and convincingly quashed by that mentality understandably inherent in the Ulster Protestant that sees in any reform a fundamental threat to their country. After three decades of violence and liberal experiment, a solution to the problem of a fundamentally divided society, a society in which fewer than 110,000 of its population of 1.5 million live in mixed Catholic and Protestant areas, is at the very least a generation away. The reforms of the 1960s and early 1970s backfired – history should have told us that too.

My upbringing as a son of the Methodist manse in the border county of lovely Fermanagh informed my attitude to the Northern Ireland problem. I have always been conscious of my Irishness, born as I was in a part of Northern Ireland where, in the thirties, the population was more or less equally divided between Protestants and Catholics, and where the two communities existed side by side in reasonable harmony on a 'live and let live' basis. It was a place where Irishness and Britishness overlapped, where English was spoken, but with the Irish idiom.

1

FERMANAGH AND
EARLY INFLUENCES

I STEPPED IT OUT RECENTLY on a soft, drizzly day in Pettigo: it is sixty paces from the front door of the old Presbyterian manse in which I was born in June 1928 to the brackish, fussy, narrow waters of the Termon river, which separates Northern Ireland from the Irish Free State, as it was called at the time of the partition of Ireland in 1921, and continued to be so called in the North for many decades.

The larger part of Pettigo is in County Donegal in the Republic of Ireland. The Northern Ireland part, known as Tullyhommon, is in County Fermanagh in the Six Counties. Another thirty paces over a short, narrow bridge and you are standing in the Republic in front of a depressing memorial erected to four young IRA volunteers 'Killed by the British Forces on the 4th June 1922'. They were Patrick Flood,

Bernard McCanny, William Kearney and William Deasley. Heroes perhaps, depending on your point of view. Born on the Tullyhommon side, I am a British citizen with about 180 feet to spare.

My father was ordained a Methodist minister in 1923. Before then he had been in Ballineen, west Cork. Following his marriage in 1924 he was sent to the Castlebar and Mayo Mission, a circuit scattered over a wide expanse of country. He soon discovered the dispiriting nature of his honeymoon appointment. A congregation of seldom more than about ten souls in his little chapel in Castlebar (now an Elim Tabernacle) on a Sunday did little to fuel his missionary zeal or the imperative of the ordination charge so recently laid upon him: to go out into all the world and preach the Gospel. Keeping in touch with the Methodists in outlying areas meant conducting open-air services on market days in the small towns round about. Colleagues from neighbouring circuits would assist: their efforts were not universally appreciated and on occasion attracted violent hostility.

But he would have had ringing in his ears the verse of one of Charles Wesley's hymns:

> O for a trumpet voice
> On all the world to call
> To bid their hearts rejoice
> In Him who died for all.

A trumpet voice would have been wasted on the Mayo air so far as the Methodist variety of the Gospel was concerned, and after eighteen months my father appealed to the Stationing Committee of the Methodist Church to rescue him from the frustration and isolation of a moribund Methodist cause in that part of Catholic Ireland. The committee responded by sending him in 1927 up-country to Pettigo, a village arguably more isolated than the town of Castlebar.

Pettigo was one of a number of villages in south Ulster that as a result of the political geography of the 1920s had found themselves on the border between the Republic and Northern Ireland. The links between the old parish of Pettigo and its natural and historic hinterland in west Fermanagh were disrupted to the extent that it is now one of the most remote areas on the border. Although its population has never risen above a few hundred people, its claim to fame is that it is the nearest village to Lough Derg, being about four miles from the point of embarkation for St Patrick's Purgatory (or Station Island, as it is more commonly called), a place of pilgrimage since the early Middle Ages which over the centuries has acquired a European significance.

Pettigo village is about 100 miles from Belfast and 130 miles from Dublin. It nestles among low hills on three sides. One comes upon it suddenly. Prior to partition in 1921, the area of the village that lies in County Donegal had been predominantly Protestant and Unionist, but soon after, with tension mounting at the time of the civil war, and harassment on both sides, the Protestants moved into Fermanagh and many Catholics crossed to the Donegal side.

The Methodist manse in Pettigo had at that time been commandeered as an urgently required police station on the Northern Ireland side of the border and it remained under police control until a purpose-built police station became available in 1937. During this period the Methodist minister lived in the Presbyterian manse, which at that time was unoccupied. It was in an insanitary condition and, being near the river, rat-infested. Once when my father was opening a trunk a rat jumped out. He was a man possessed of unfailing cheerfulness, and his worst response, by way of an oath, would have been a mild 'bad scran to it!', the derivation of which I have never been able to discover.

The Presbyterians, however, contributed towards improving the house, as also did the Stormont government which also paid the Methodist Church an 'inferiority rent' in recompense for having displaced their minister into the Presbyterian manse. In 1928, the year I was born, the government offered to buy the appropriated manse outright for £850. The offer was turned down and the house was subsequently restored to the Methodist Church.

Under the itinerate system operating in those days, a Methodist clergyman stayed no longer than five years in one place. He was either posted to his next position by the Methodist Conference or invited by a congregation to replace its departing minister. The system was mutually advantageous. On the one hand it meant that a man who was uncomfortable and not in harmony with his congregation could move on fairly quickly and hopefully to more agreeable pastures. On the other, a congregation not happy with its minister was not saddled with him indefinitely, as is the case with the clergy of other denominations. Until I was sixteen we moved around Lough Erne – Newtownbutler, Brookeborough and Irvinestown – never far from the border.

My father, a popular minister throughout County Fermanagh, was never without an invitation. He was a talented musician, a fine pianist with a pleasing baritone voice. He was articulate, friendly, maddeningly unambitious, with a keen sense of humour. His sermons were well-researched, central and relevant to Christian teaching. I have the small case in which he kept them and I would judge that they are as relevant today as when he first prepared them.

My childhood days in the Fermanagh of the thirties were happy, healthy, carefree and secure, lived in those villages around Lough Erne. My earliest memories are of waking up on spring mornings to the song of birds in the apple trees in full blossom in the manse gardens. In later years the line 'With it the blackbird breaks the young day's heart' by the poet Patmore wonderfully evoked the poignancy of those childhood spring mornings.

As in Goldsmith's 'Sweet Auburn' further south in County Westmeath, where that poet first went to school, spring seemed to come early. I remember summers for their nights full of the call of the corncrake, now almost extinct, their habitats destroyed as meadows fall victim to modern farming techniques. It was an out-of-doors childhood. We played hounds and hares, a more spacious form of hide and seek, over the endless small fields. Along hedgerow paths we went bird-nesting. A strong catapult, made from discarded motor tyre tubes, was a prized possession, as well as the more inaccurate sling made from two leather boot thongs attached to a small oval leather launching pad. The most skilful could send stones probably over two hundred yards. The sling, with the stone in the leather pouch at the end, would be whirled round vigorously and at the precise moment one could achieve the maximum revolutions, the loose thong held between thumb and forefinger would be released, hurling the stone on its way. I was satisfied that David's astonishing accuracy in striking Goliath plum on the forehead just under his helmet with the first stone could only be ascribed to divine intervention – which I suppose the biblical account would have me believe. True, Goliath did present a large target, being ten and a half feet tall. But on any showing it was an unbelievable shot with what seemed a basically inaccurate weapon. I discovered later that in David's day the sling could be used with almost mathematical precision: the Book of Judges (20:16) informed me that 'Among all this people there were seven hundred chosen [Hebrew] men left-handed; every one could sling stones at a hairs breadth, and not miss'! Somewhere else I read that shepherds could turn their flocks in the desired direction by slinging stones close to the noses of the leading sheep.

Another of our activities, which would scarcely escape the attention of the authorities now, was experimenting with a small homemade horizontal mortar. Some granules of carbide (used to provide acetylene gas for bicycle lamps) were placed in an empty Tate and Lyle syrup tin, the base of which had been pierced. Wetting the carbide with spittle released the gas; when the lid was firmly replaced and a lighted match was applied to the hole, the lid was blown off some distance with a most satisfactory bang.

In July 1934, we left Newtownbutler and moved twelve miles away to the Methodist manse in the one-street village of Brookeborough. Manses were furnished throughout, so a small removal van was adequate to remove the few possessions we had. At that time a Methodist minister was paid £250 a year – a stipend that my mother, with careful management, made go remarkably far. The Sunday chicken was still doing duty as soup at the end of the week. Clothes handed down from one child to the other and stout boots helped to keep down family expenditure. Our needs were modest and life was simple.

Paddy Healey must have regretted the day we arrived. His public house, outwardly and visibly unchanged to this day (carried on by the present licensee as 'the Brokenspoke'), was separated from the manse by the entry to the manse yard and garden beyond. On the other side was the Brookeborough Orange Hall, then the tiny post office run by tiny Miss West whose Christmas parties I shall always remember. Letters posted with her were guaranteed to reach Santa Claus in good time.

These were the days of the Band of Hope, the temperance movement and exhortations to sign the pledge. My mother regarded the tasting or touching of strong drink as a mortal sin. Public houses were totally destructive of society and should not be allowed to exist. She gave Paddy Healey a hard time during our five years in Brookeborough. Fortunately for them, O'Donnell's and Lavell's public houses further up the street were outside her range.

Paddy was driven to conduct some of his business by way of signs and signals. Jimmy Kenny, caretaker of the courthouse on the other side of the manse, lived directly opposite us; in order to avoid my mother seeing him entering Paddy's pub, Jimmy would often come to his door and indicate the coming evening's requirement of porter to Paddy across the street by means of a show of fingers on the door post.

The expectations of the wandering down-and-outs who came to the manse door and, with one eye on Paddy Healey's pub, asked for money to buy food enough to relieve the pangs of hunger were invariably unrealised. When offered a good square meal by my mother, these wanderers would turn sadly, often indignantly, away.

The closeness of the pub to the manse ensured a pervasive smell of porter. That, and the effluent from the washing of bottles seeping into a drain that ran from the pub into the manse garden, kept the problem very much alive. I can well remember the frequent maudlin strains of 'Annie Laurie' issuing from the pub, from the voice of Brew Scott, the big husky local layabout. I cannot remember him singing anything else.

One incident in which Brew came to grief was unforgettable. He was the worse for drink on a day I was sent over to Andy Morrow's shop on the other side of the street to fetch a plain white loaf. Andy was one of three village grocers, all members of the Methodist Church, between whom my mother felt obliged to share the manse patronage. He was a timid, effete man, who on one occasion complained of the communion wine being too strong (Methodist communion wine then was weak blackcurrant juice). Also in the shop at the time was Cecil Johnston, the local dairy farmer. Brew, with the drink in and the wit out, said something uncomplimentary about Cecil's wife. The fight that followed was fierce and one-sided. I stood transfixed, while Andy escaped into his house through the door behind the counter. I remember well the sight of Brew Scott when it was all over: one black-and-blue eye closed, bleeding from the nose and cut about the face. Utterly unruffled, Cecil Johnston got up into his cart, took up the reins, geed-up the horse and, with one Wellington boot placed on the side baffleboard, made his way down the street towards his farm on the outskirts of the village, in a manner that seemed to say, 'A man's got to do what a man's got to do.' The police didn't bother too much about that sort of thing in those days in a small village.

My mother laid any violence there was in the village at Paddy Healey's door. As she did when a little old lady got very drunk in his pub, went up the street and threw a stone through the window of Elliott's shop, Elliott being another of 'our' grocers. The woman was arrested, and lodged in a police cell. When this came to my mother's ears later in the day she went down to the police station and advised Sergeant Bowman in no uncertain terms that he had arrested the wrong person. It should have been Paddy Healey. She demanded the release of the prisoner from the cell, brought her back to the manse, and gave her a meal and shelter for the night.

The smell of Guinness has forever been associated for me with Paddy Healey's pub. I have never to this day been able to bring myself to drink it.

Further up the street, past the large-wheeled village pump which we used when pipes were frozen in winter, was the public elementary school with its two classrooms. Master Cameron, the principal, was an avuncular, lazy, chain-smoking man who did not seem to possess the energy to draw on his cigarettes which he left smouldering between his lips, each length of ash falling of its own weight. This seemed a terrible waste of a cigarette. How I wished he would occasionally take a puff and blow out some smoke. He spent a considerable part of the school day chatting with passers-by in the street outside. He was in no hurry. There was plenty of time.

Cameron's main interests were fishing, butterflies and birds. We often used to see him and his son, Ivan, cycling towards Lough Erne on fishing expeditions. He preferred trout wet-fly fishing. His soft-checked trilby hat was festooned with a variety of brightly coloured flies for all seasons and conditions of river and lake. No bream, perch, pike, trout or roach was safe from him in the stretch of water where he settled down for a day's fishing.

On his desk was an array of butterflies and moths pinned and identified on cards. In the coal bunker, just outside the classroom door, there often cowered an owl or kestrel hawk which some of us had captured and brought in. Furnishings on the classroom wall included a large thirty-two-county map of Ireland, a pre-partition relic. It seemed of vital importance that a knowledge of geography included the whereabouts of the principal towns of each of the thirty-two counties: Athy, Kildare, Naas, Maynooth; Longford, Granard and Edgeworthstown; Meath, Trim, Navan, Kells. For some reason or another the principal towns of the northern counties did not seem to stick with me. They were far away up north and not somewhere I was likely often to be.

Excursions to the seaside were across the border to Bundoran or Rossnowlagh in Donegal. Frequent journeys in and out of the Republic meant stopping at the customs post and having the car triptyque, or *laissez-passer*, stamped, but to me both sides of the border were the same Ireland, the place in which I lived. On occasion, we tuned into Athlone for Radio Éireann programmes. It was never pointed out that the Republic was politically a foreign country. As a child I would not have understood. So I suppose, if I had ever been asked, I would have said I was Irish. I knew I was not English.

The Silver Jubilee of King George and Queen Mary, celebrated in 1935, when schoolchildren received a thin tin of black chocolates, the lid decorated with a colourful King and Queen in royal regalia, provided a very agreeable reminder that I was British as well and that there was an empire of which their majesties symbolised the unity. That day there was a splendid picnic for the entire village at Sir Basil Brooke's residence at nearby Ashbrooke.

Everything that was marked 'British made' was superior. Toys from Japan, China or Czechoslovakia were inferior in every way. Through cigarette cards we saw the best of British: footballers, cricketers, tennis players, motor cars and ships of the British navy.

Once a year, on the Twelfth of July, to celebrate the chasing of the Papist James from the banks of the Boyne by the Protestant William, we confirmed our loyalty to the Crown by thrusting a Union Jack out of a bedroom window, jamming it between the sash and the framework. We were careful not to get it upside down, a common enough mistake due to the complications of the flag but one that often attracted the attention of the police who would require that the flag be put the right way up.

We watched the Brookeborough flute band and Orange lodge as they marched from the Boer War Memorial at the top of the street the three hundred yards to the Clogher Valley railway station at the bottom, with Jim Kenny (the twenty-seven-year-old son of the care-taker of the courthouse), who had Down's Syndrome, walking importantly alongside the big drum at a safe arm's length. At the station the marchers entrained in a 'special' for the Field at Maguiresbridge, five miles away. The Field was awash with orange collarettes and sashes and the colourful uniforms of bandsmen. I was led to believe that to be a true Orangeman that day you had to eat one of the petals of an orange lily. Thinking about this I would take one between finger and thumb, but I was not prepared to take it any further.

The Clogher Valley Railway, which served the farming community in those days, covered a distance of thirty-seven miles from its western terminal at Maguiresbridge in Fermanagh to Tynan in County Armagh, through Brookeborough, Fivemiletown, Augher, Clogher, Aughnacloy and Caledon. The steam tramway-type engines were each fitted with a huge headlamp, a cow-catcher and hinged flaps over the wheels to protect animals from getting caught up with the train in motion. These engines lent a Wild West look to Fivemiletown as they and their coaches, which had small covered platforms at both ends, steamed heavily down the centre of the narrow main street. To ensure safety, the engine ran backwards as there was a better view from the cab in that position. On busy days, like the Twelfth of July, I can remember seeing some wagons fitted up with benches to accommodate extra pas-sengers. These specials often needed two engines and sometimes three to get them over some of the longer and higher hills. The names of three engines come to mind: Erne, Caledon and Errigal. Standing nearby as one of these monsters came rushing menacingly through a gap in the hedge, across the road, and disappeared among the hedgerows and bushes on the other side was a fearsome thing to a small boy.

Catholics and Protestants lived peaceably side by side in Fermanagh in the 1930s. As children we knew nothing of the riots that sporadically erupted in Belfast. We were unaware of the battles of York Street and Lancaster Street, when animosities nurtured over centuries came to the surface with much injury and loss of life. We knew more about the Spanish Civil War and about the invasion of Abyssinia by Mussolini, which we learned of from the *Children's Newspaper* which my parents encouraged us three boys to read. Emperor Haile Selassie, the Lion of Judah, was a hero. We knew more about the plight of his country than the violence in our own. A rhyme at that time (sung to the tune of 'Roll Along, Covered Wagon, Roll Along') comes to mind:

> Will you come to Abyssinia, will you come?
> Bring your own ammunition and a gun;
> Mussolini will be there, firing bullets in the air,
> Will you come to Abyssinia, will you come?

Jim and Tommy McCusker, who were two of the several Catholics at Master Cameron's school, would no doubt have joined us in any expeditionary adventure into Abyssinia. They lived down the street in a house built for ex-servicemen. Their father had fought and was wounded in World War One. The last time I saw Jim was on the platform of Omagh station in September 1941: I was on my way back to school in Belfast and he was in the uniform of a rating of the Royal Navy.

School days in Fermanagh brought me into daily contact with Catholic boys and girls who seemed in no way different from me. Almost all schooling was sectarian, but in those days before school buses, Protestant and Catholic children who lived in outlying areas attended their local primary school whether it was Catholic or Protestant. Years in the same class and general school contacts undoubtedly gave an ease of relationship and sometimes resulted in long-standing friendships. Yet only a small proportion of children in Northern Ireland came into close contact at school with any other than their coreligionists.

The nationalist community were not likely to forget Sir Basil Brooke's observations in Derry in March 1934 that he had not lost a night's sleep over his earlier speeches in which he had recommended people 'not to employ Catholics as their religion was so politically minded that they were out to destroy us as a body'. Although Catholics and Protestants in Fermanagh lived together on relatively good terms, resentment was never far below the surface – not surprisingly.

The story is told that Sir Basil Brooke, regarded by the *Impartial Reporter* of the time as 'the best-hated member of the Ulster government by the patriots of the true state and the nationalists of Northern Ireland', was fishing once offshore in Lough Erne, which is notorious for its soft mud and unsure footing, when he got into difficulties. Three small boys playing nearby rushed to his rescue and brought him ashore, pulled off his waders and made him comfortable on the bank. Overcome with gratitude he asked the boys did they know who he was. No, they didn't.

'Well,' he said, 'I am Sir Basil Brooke, minister of agriculture for Northern Ireland, and because of what you have done I would like to give each one of you something to remember this occasion ... What would you like?' he asked one of the boys.

'I've always wanted a bicycle. My father could never afford to buy me one,' he replied.

'You shall have it, next week,' the gentleman replied. 'And how about you?' he asked the next boy.

'I would like a fishing rod.'

'I'll see that you are sent one as soon as possible. And you?' he asked the remaining youngster.

'I would like a state fun-e-ral, sorr.'

'A state funeral?'

'Yes, sorr, for when I get home and my fether finds out who I've pult out of the lake he'll kill me!'

Whether true or false, the story points up the underlying bitterness that existed amongst Catholics. It was reflected within my knowledge on other occasions. Cottage meetings were important centres of religious worship for Protestant country folk. On the last Tuesday of each month the Gilmores of Conacrea, near Irvinestown, arranged for my father to hold meetings in their large farmhouse. After the service in the living room (attended by all the main Protestant denominations), Miss Gilmore would invite the congregation to the back kitchen which by then smelled deliciously of fresh bread, buttermilk, goldies and sowans (porridges made from maize and oats respectively). The 'serving man', John Weir, a deep-dyed republican employed on the Gilmores' farm, would come into the kitchen at this point in the fellowship and was often heard to say mournfully over a cup of tea with a cut of Miss Gilmore's wheaten bread in his other hand, 'Sorry will I be the day I have to shoot my neighbours.'

From an early age we Protestant children picked up some pretty offensive sentiments, portending a drastic doom for the Catholics, such as:

> Slitter, slaughter
> Holy Water!
> Sprinkle the Papishes every one!
> And that's what we'll do
> And we'll cut them in two,
> And the Protestant boys'll carry the drum.

This would no doubt have been chanted with more vehemence in Sandy Row in Belfast than in the small villages of Fermanagh. To have repeated this in the hearing of my parents would have meant at the least a severe scolding. They would not have tolerated sectarian abuse of any kind.

Unlike the clergy of the Presbyterian Church and the Church of Ireland few, if any, Methodist ministers were members of the Orange Order. The Orange Order was established as an essential bulwark in the defence of Protestant interests, its members standing shoulder to shoulder to advance the cause of loyalty, liberty and religion. It was not only a Protestant organisation, but also anti-Catholic, as it had every right to be, given the natural religious hatred and long, turbulent history of Catholic and Protestant relationships. Methodist clergy preferred to parade their orthodoxy in the lives they lived, in the first place to serve their age and fulfil their calling by expounding the Bible and the Christian faith and then, and only then, to offer these principles to the individuals to whom they were preaching. They brought a simple message of individual salvation, forgiveness and redemption in line with the paramount Wesleyan theme that 'all men can be saved and saved to the uttermost'.

As Nonconformists, Methodists came to be viewed by the established Church of Ireland as of doubtful political stability, as suspect as Catholics. Being all things to all men made them the soft underbelly of Protestantism. The prevailing attitude of Methodist clergy to Catholics was that our differences were not as important as what we had in common.

In 1934, my father was invited to preach at an Orange service – in the grounds of the Church of Ireland rectory outside Brookeborough. The only man present not wearing a sash, he chose for his text one that appeared on many Orange banners: 'Honour all men, Love the brotherhood, Fear God, Honour the King'. The injunction 'Love the brotherhood' would have been a bit tricky. 'Brotherhood' in the eyes of some might have been thought of as synonymous with the order of which he was not a member. He did not subscribe to the Protestant ethic that diluted Christian love into patriotism, loyalty to friends and industriousness. However that may be, my father told me that after the service, Sir Basil Brooke came up to him, slapped him on the back and said, 'Brother McIvor, that was a great statement!'

Years afterwards, when Sir Basil Brooke had become Lord Brookeborough and I was a Unionist MP, I found myself sitting next to the great man at a function in the members' dining room at Stormont. Desperate for something to get me off the ground I mentioned the occasion when my father, whom I described as a non-Orangeman, addressed the Orange service in Brookeborough. I drew a blank. He responded with an accommodating smile which did not seem to reach the hooded eyes.

The outbreak of war saw our family in Irvinestown. On nearby Lough Erne, Shorts Sunderland flying boats and American Catalinas were gathering to patrol the Western Approaches. Despite formal neutrality the Irish Free State cooperated with Britain to solve the problem of access to the Atlantic. In January 1941, to deal with the U-boat menace, de Valera gave permission for Allied aircraft to overfly Donegal Bay so long as flights were kept at a 'good height' and they avoided flying over the Irish military port of Finner. This was a major breakthrough in Anglo-Irish relations at the time – though the arrangements were kept a close secret. It was to be discovered later that many convoys of British shipping were doomed not because of the Free State's refusal to make available its ports to Britain but because the cipher used to encode U-boat communications was unexpectedly changed from the Enigma cipher which had been broken by Britain's cryptanalysts.

A navigator in one of the Sunderlands, Derek Seymour, would come to the manse to sleep off a forty-eight-hour stint of duty over the Atlantic. In civilian life he was a church organist. He often took me with him to St McCartan's cathedral in Enniskillen where he had permission to practise on the organ there. This was my earliest introduction to a large church organ. In later years I was to be invited to deputise for organists in some Belfast city churches.

The Irvinestown Local Defence Volunteers (the LDV – uncharitably called the 'Look, Duck and Vanish brigade') quickly mobilised in defence of the town. At a time when the Home Guard in England were still training with broom handles, these volunteers were able to produce rifles, originally smuggled into Larne in 1912 from the *Clyde-valley* to arm loyalists in the fight against Home Rule – 'pikes in the thatch'. On the barrel of each rifle was an oval plate inscribed 'For God and Ulster'.

In September 1940 my close association with Fermanagh ended when I went off to the Methodist College in Belfast as a boarder.

Methody, as it is known, was a godsend to the children of Methodist ministers, whose education tended to be insecure and disrupted. As there were not many secondary schools in Northern Ireland outside Belfast, Methody gave children of the manse a chance they would not have had elsewhere.

The school was established to serve two needs: as a college in which students would be trained for the ministry of the Methodist Church, and as a grammar school for the sons and daughters of Methodist ministers and of ministers of other denominations. Foundation scholarships were provided. The scholarship places made available for sons and daughters of the manses were treated with some suspicion by the education authorities, and it was often necessary to demonstrate that awards were not being made too freely. So, in order to attract the education grant, the school would hold its own internal qualifying examination. There is no record of anyone having failed this test.

Belfast was reached by boarding the Bundoran Express train at Irvinestown and changing at Bundoran Junction for Omagh to catch the Londonderry–Belfast train. The Bundoran Express hardly lived up to its name. Its circuitous route via Dundalk, Clones, Enniskillen and Pettigo, Belleek and Ballyshannon precluded anything in the way of high speed. Its primary function seems to have been to encourage Dubliners to spend their holidays at the Donegal seaside resort of Bundoran, where the Great Northern just happened to own an hotel. At Pettigo it would drop off pilgrims to Lough Derg. A bizarre consequence of the Republic of Ireland not following the UK in introducing daylight saving time (double summer time) during World War Two was that you could arrive by train in Pettigo at the same time as you had left Enniskillen!

I had been plucked from the comforts of home and the abundance and freedom of life in Fermanagh to the cheerlessness of a boarding school in wartime Belfast, and for some time I found it a painful, tearful experience. We lived in almost unrelieved gloom. Dormitories were blacked-out by thick black paper pasted over the windows. At night, windows were hermetically closed, and only then could the light be switched on. Unremitting austerities, in particular food rationing, involved meticulous weighing and measuring – a meagre two ounces of butter per week and about three times that amount of margarine.

At least the air raids were an exciting distraction. The blackout was the most irksome wartime discipline. Because of it, school societies ceased to function except in a limited way after school. As secretary of the Current Affairs Society, I remember once giving a paper on Stalin's revolutionary Five Year Plan and system of collective farms which I assured my audience had made a dramatic improvement to the quality of life in Russia. Grotesquely, both in the media and in public opinion, Stalin was now 'Uncle Joe', a benevolent dictator, and of more relevance than Northern Ireland's political problems which were by now in cold storage – people had other things on their minds.

It is a matter of some shame that we had little or no contact with the Catholic grammar schools in Belfast. The first time St Malachy's swam into my ken was an occasion when we played them at water polo at the Falls Baths, later on in my time at Methody. They did not play rugby, so we did not meet them in that context. St Malachy's and St Mary's Christian Brothers School did not impinge on our consciousness because of the system of segregation of Catholic and Protestant schools. It so happened that later I was to have the opportunity of making a personal visit to St Malachy's. I had been taken ill during my Senior Certificate examinations and had missed my French oral. It was arranged I should take it at St Malachy's when I recovered. I recollect the kindness and courtesy with which I was shown around the school by Father John McMullan, the president, as if I were some important guest. He knew that Greek was one of my subjects, and I remember him enthusiastically reflecting on the properties of the Greek participle – its flexible qualities. This was a refinement completely beyond me, so I just nodded in agreement. It made me feel important that he would speak like this to a very average schoolboy.

The general desperate enthusiasm for the defeat of Germany was not totally shared by the Catholic community. We knew at school that there was an unemployment problem amongst Catholics in Belfast which should not have existed in view of the large amount of wartime manufacturing work available. The explanation given was that Catholic workers dragged their feet (in the way we expected them to, I suppose), not willing to put their shoulders to the wheel in the interests of the war effort. And politics emerged very briefly once in Ronald Marshall's history class. Ronnie, as we called him, was a tall blond elegant man, a likely stand-in for Alec Guinness in *Our Man in Havana* in tropical suit and panama hat. Niall Rudd, a lifelong friend of my school days, sometime Professor of Latin at Bristol University, in his autobiography *Pale Green, Light Orange* describes Ronnie as a Yorkshire caterpillar that had gone through the chrysalis of London University and emerged as a cosmopolitan butterfly. It was when we were studying John Buchan's *Prester John* that he raised the reality of the religious divide in Northern Ireland. I cannot remember the context but in one of his amusing asides he declared that 'the Pope was just about as popular in Blaauwildebeestefontein as he is in Portadown'. Up to then I had not been aware of the significance of Portadown as a Protestant stronghold.

I had inherited from my father some talent as a pianist. In 1942 and 1944 I was awarded the third and second prizes respectively at the Belfast Musical Festival – in the 1944 festival I missed first place by one point, according to the adjudicators. Ronnie, who was the senior housemaster and head of the English department, was a classical music addict. After lights out we could hear him gamely struggling with Chopin in his room down the corridor. When he asked me to play with him two-piano arrangements of some Mozart and Bach, I was scarcely likely to refuse. We had many tense sessions together on the two upright pianos in the Castlereagh houseroom. Exchanges of 'Sorry!' were as frequent as the mutual apologies of golfers in a foursome who keep putting each other in bunkers or deep rough. Disaster was never far away and it was highly satisfactory, and something of a victory, when we finished together.

I liked Ronnie and would not have wished to fall from grace in his eyes. But it was too late when one afternoon I heard the precise, light footsteps coming tap tap along the corridor towards my cubicle. I had just time enough to flick the casual cigarette I was enjoying towards the open window that looked out on the spire of Elmwood Presbyterian church. My aim was poor. The cigarette landed in the middle of the coiled rope ladder provided for our safety in case the dormitory went on fire, at the same time as Ronnie arrived to ask if we could arrange a piano session. We both looked at the thin blue ascending stream of smoke. There was a moment of silence, then 'McIvor, are you going stawk, staiwing, waiving mad?' – he had difficulty with his Rs – and with that he turned on his heel and walked off. I reckoned our fraught performance of Mozart and Bach were at an end there and then. Our pianistic relationship was soon restored, however, and we resumed our battles.

The time arrived when I had to decide what to do with my life. I envied those who had outstanding strengths and aptitudes that would inform their choices. For me there were no clear pointers. My father was keen that none of his three boys should choose law. He often quoted Dr Johnson's observation that 'he never would wish to speak ill of a man behind his back, but he understood the gentleman to be an attorney'. It was hoped by my father that I would follow in his footsteps, but I had no sense of vocation for the Church – and I had had enough of the accompanying domestic stringencies.

The photograph of an uncle in full fig as a Dublin barrister in the early twenties had always occupied a prominent place at home. As well as fancying myself in wig and gown, I also believed that the legal profession might satisfy a streak of independence in me, and although I knew nothing about that profession I nevertheless made up my mind to become a lawyer and study for the Bar. In those days there was little competition for university places. Entrance qualifications were based on the results of the Senior Certificate. Queen's University was in favour of a wide range of subjects for Senior Certificate and I was able to satisfy the Faculty of Law in English, Modern History, Latin, Greek, French and subsidiary Mathematics. I had just turned seventeen. My birthday falling in June meant I was a year younger than most in my year.

Methody had a reputation for academic excellence in the unique selection system of education in Northern Ireland and we were pushed pretty hard. I look back on the school with much affection and gratitude. It was magnificent schooling, and I owe a lot to the teaching there. If a pupil had any kind of talent in any kind of sphere, he or she was given the chance and the encouragement to use it. A whole treasure house of English and classical literature was opened up to me, cultivating a love for reading which has enriched my life.

2

THE WORLD OF LAW

THE DEAN OF THE FACULTY OF LAW at Queen's University, Professor J.L. Montrose, a large, ample man with tight grey curls, cherubic face, deep blue eyes and trembling chin, looked past me out through the window of his room in Elmwood House (which then housed the three departments of Law, Economics and Political Science) and meditated out loud:

> Seven hours to sleep
> To Law's grave study seven
> Ten to the world allot
> And all to heaven.

I supposed this was a not unreasonable allocation of one's time, but having just been emancipated from the restraints of boarding-school life I could not see myself giving any undertaking to keep to the disciplined regime suggested by those lofty lines.

Professor Montrose noted that I had taken Greek and asked me had I read Plato's *Republic* in the Greek. I had not. He did not think that Homer's *Iliad* which described so graphically the chasing of Achilles by Hector around the walls of Troy was any substitute for a serious book by Plato (and in Greek). He asked did I not think seventeen was on the young side for university – did I not agree that I should go back to school for an upper sixth year, sort out the weaknesses in order to prepare myself for a totally new and demanding discipline? No I did not.

Montrose was a kind man at heart, and against his better judgement he admitted me as a student in October 1945. I am sure he was right at the time that an extra year at school would have benefited me academically. But in the long run it was not to make a difference to how things would turn out. Things are meant to be.

I was enrolled at Queen's and, having decided to go for the Bar, was duly admitted as a student into the Honourable Society of the Inn of Court of Northern Ireland. It cost my parents £25 in stamp duty, which I knew they could ill afford.

After the war, life was full of hope. Demand for graduates was high, their supply limited. A degree was a passport to a job. Today the unprecedented expansion of university places has seen the evaporation of that market. Students at the Faculty of Law at Queen's at that time would scarcely have numbered one hundred. Most of us could realistically expect to find a place in business, the civil service or the professions. That is, if we were Protestant. Deep down I was aware that when it would come to the bit, in terms of a career, Protestants had a head start over Catholics. It was not a level playing field. So far as I was concerned that was the way things were. I hope I never took this into my calculations – I don't think I did.

Catholic and Protestant students were enrolled in about equal numbers in the faculty. They had come from a segregated system of education in which Catholic children were educated in Catholic maintained schools and Protestants were educated in state (*de facto* Protestant) schools. They had had no opportunities to meet during school days. We integrated without problem and related to one another perfectly naturally, as we would have done during our school days had we been given the chance. Moreover, as students of law we were less likely to be concerned with issues of religious or tribal affiliation. The practice of the law would recognise no barriers of creed or culture. The law was an elite profession, and for the Catholic students, becoming members of it gave them the chance of upward mobility into the higher reaches of a society in which religious discrimination in the workplace was entrenched.

In those days a student's main objective was to obtain a university degree as quickly and painlessly as possible. This was most certainly not what a university was for in Montrose's view. As embryonic lawyers the pursuit of truth should be our main concern and high calling. Is there an objective truth to follow? – is there a golden thread of truth to be discovered in all aspects of the law? – what is truth? these were all matters that were going to complicate the task of providing a crisp answer to examination questions.

Montrose pitched aspirations impossibly high, although it was known that his judgements on examinations were merciful. He would strive mightily to push a student over the borderline into a higher class of degree in the face of opposition from external examiners. But stretching minds was his paramount duty. The net result was that it was impossible to take notes on his lectures that made sense. He had a mumbling delivery and was short on communication skills. Far more important, he laboured to stimulate our critical faculties.

During the Nuremberg Trials of November 1945 he held a seminar to discuss under what authority that court was set up. He suggested that the Nuremberg Trials were vengeance cooked up by the victors, without any respectable basis in international law; that by their own saturation bombing of Dresden and Hamburg in February 1945, causing thousands of civilian deaths at a time when Germany was collapsing, and by the atom-bombing of Hiroshima and Nagasaki when Japan was losing the war in South East Asia, the Allies had lost any moral authority to conduct such proceedings. The voicing of these doubts was at the time courageous. The general public was satisfied that Nazi war criminals should be eliminated from the earth. The arguments around the trial of war criminals are very much alive today. The hangings at Nuremberg have not deterred subsequent murderous regimes.

Mock trials were an important part of the learning process. I remember one presided over by Professor Francis Newark in full fig as a High Court judge, held in Court Number 1 in Crumlin Road courthouse. I was counsel for the defence in borrowed wig, gown and bands. In the front row of the student jury, seated second from my right, was a stunningly attractive dark-haired girl. I cannot remember the nature of the charges against my client, whether he was found guilty or acquitted, but I do remember the girl – Jill Anderson – whom I subsequently married.

In the immediate post-war years the Literary and Scientific Society of Queen's University (the Literific) was the forum for undergraduate debating. Orange and Green topics were only very occasionally substantive motions for debate, but it became customary for these to be raised by speakers from the floor, however irrelevant they were to the main discussion – an opportunity for light-hearted undergraduate banter. Our horizons were dreadfully limited. On occasions some of these mischievous interpolations would get out of hand, especially when a number of latecomers had joined the proceedings straight from a neighbouring pub. Amidst all the clowning and comedy, however, one was aware at times of the presence of committed ideologues, ranging from such Unionist and Orange extremists as Tom Teevan, a law student, to genuinely liberal and humane nationalists such as a lecturer, Jimmy Scott, later a professor in the Department of Dentistry. The cut and thrust of Orange-and-Green confrontations was sterile, puerile and conducted at a very low level.

Tom Teevan, a brilliant student who gained a first-class honours degree in law, was chairman of the Law Society, president of the Literific, and chairman of the Unionist Association at Queen's. A member of the Orange and Black orders, an Apprentice Boy, and, at twenty-one, chairman of the Limavady Urban Council, he was a vigorous champion of the Crown and the British Empire. He turned loyalty into a new political *ism*: loyalism. I often wondered whether he really took himself or his subject seriously at all with so much of the absurd in his performances. Wearing a laurel wreath and boxing gloves he was received in triumph in west Belfast that rainy night in 1950 he won the Westminster seat with a majority of 913 over J. Beattie, Eire Labour – a close-run thing. At twenty-three he was the youngest MP at Westminster. I found him a warm, impish character. He was well loved amongst his peers, renowned for good companionship, with innumerable friends of all creeds and classes. Sadly, he died at the age of twenty-seven, then a practising barrister.

A close friend of mine, Oliver McKeague, a moderate if rather orthodox Catholic, became president of the Literific. He and Brian Baird, the honorary secretary (with whom I had been at Methody), visited Dublin to discuss an invitation to Sean MacBride (minister of external affairs and amongst the most prominent of IRA leaders in the 1920s and 1930s) to come to Queen's to speak to the Literific. MacBride, who was to become a Nobel Peace Prize winner in 1974, was the leader of Clann na Poblachta, a charismatic figure who excited great interest and enthusiasm, particularly among liberal intellectuals in the student population of University College Dublin. When the authorities at Queen's learned of the invitation they informed the officers of the Literific that no venue for such a meeting would be made available on the university campus. A new venue was sought within Queen's on the basis of the promotion of free speech. A good deal of controversy was excited at the time both within and outside the university. It became something of a *cause célèbre*. The authorities were adamant and threatened the Literific with withdrawal of the society's grant forthwith if the meeting proceeded.

In the end, MacBride 'regretfully' withdrew his acceptance of the invitation in order to avoid further contention and embarrassment. The Literific subsequently disaffiliated from the Students' Representative Council in order to demonstrate that the university's oldest student society was still prepared to defend the principles of free speech on campus.

In 1948 I graduated from Queen's, and the following year I passed the Bar Final held at Lincoln's Inn in London of which I was a student. I was called to the Bar of Northern Ireland in January 1950, a fully fledged barrister-at-law. Not everyone, however, was to find that the reality matched expectations. I for one found that I had been accepted into a profession that soon seemed unable to deliver a secure livelihood.

The Bar Library at the Royal Courts of Justice in Belfast was a splendid place in which to work. The fine working library provided accommodation for all the sixty-six practising members of the Northern Ireland Bar that there were when I was called in 1950. The high mahogany bookshelves, which were separated by desks each accommodating four to eight beavering barristers, and the robed figures bustling in and out, lent an air of great industry and learning.

For a twenty-one-year-old tenderfoot, without money, family connection or reasonable expectations, it was quite something to be able to count amongst my colleagues the best legal brains in Northern Ireland. And I had not just a nodding acquaintanceship with these great men. There was an almost masonic brotherhood of mutual concern and assistance. A solicitor who found himself pressured to send instructions to a young unlearned novice could be certain that that young barrister would immediately seek out the most distinguished member of the library in order to pick his brains. The solicitor's client would in the end be armed with the best opinion obtainable from the Bar. As Maurice Healey, of the Irish Bar, observes in his book *The Old Munster Circuit*, 'the Library system . . . not only enabled us all to practise cheaply, but gave every neophyte three hundred tutors to teach him his business and knock the corners off him'. Rubbing shoulders day in and day out with the distinguished and fashionable counsel of the day, and discussing with them the difficulties of a case, was an insurance against disaster.

I suffered a long, penurious apprenticeship. But I had been warned beforehand how difficult it would be to establish a foothold, particularly as there was insufficient work to go round. The legal aid system had not been introduced, and there were no industrial or local tribunals, the subsequent establishment of which would increase enormously the amount of work available for barristers. Some became impatient and accepted positions in the Colonial Legal Service when there was still a British Empire requiring legally trained personnel for administrative and legal duties in far-off places. Lacking friends in the profession or contacts outside it, all I could do was as often as possible to appear robed in the Great Hall, there to be on view to solicitors. Perhaps there might be some pickings in the Motion Court. I might be lucky enough to be handed a simple ex-parte application (an emergency procedural application) on the spot in that court, often with very little time or opportunity to understand and familiarise myself with what it was about. The thing was to assume a pretence of being busy, to be seen actively and purposefully on the go, engaged in apparently serious conversation with anyone on Friday morning in that crowded hall, when solicitors would be there to instruct or attend their chosen counsel. Oh, for a smile from a solicitor. A smile of recognition could raise the hope that just maybe the bestower of the smile might at some future time follow it up with a more tangible benefaction. At the very least it might boost my self-esteem which was always in danger of being holed below the water line. At these times I remembered the chilling biblical reference equally applicable to the Bar: 'Many are called but few are chosen.'

There were barristers fortunate enough to have early opportunities to win their spurs – those who came to the Bar with a distinguished academic reputation, those who had served in the armed forces during the war and were infinitely more mature than twenty-one-year-olds like myself, and of course those with fathers or uncles in the legal profession or with relatives in business who could be influential in directing work their way. We worked in close proximity to one another and I could judge the relative success of my colleagues. It was a long cruel walk from the door of the car park down to the other end of the library where my desk was. It was depressing of a morning to run the gauntlet of desks piled high with brown envelopes, fearful that my close competitors in the library who had received that work had the solicitors, the source of the work, completely tied in. Eventually I began to receive what were really goodwill briefs and from the most unexpected quarters. One came from a solicitor unknown to me who greeted me on one occasion with, 'I knew your father well as a young man. I used to play the organ in his church.' But none of these complimentary briefs were intended or could be expected to hold any promise for the future. I made forty guineas my first year, supplementing my income by reporting cases and writing some things for the *Irish Law Times* at one guinea for the first column and seven shillings and sixpence for each column thereafter. It was hard work and badly paid, but in other respects valuable.

My parents had moved to Lurgan and I lived with them, so my expenses consisted mainly of travelling between Lurgan and Belfast. Every Saturday during the season, I turned out for the Lurgan Rugby xv, travelling to Dungannon, Armagh, Magherafelt, Donaghadee, Lisburn, Banbridge, Dromore, Larne, Portadown or to Belfast clubs. I was able to finance the expenses incurred out of fees, but was very far from being in a financial position to marry, which I did nevertheless in January 1953 at Lambeg parish church, on an overdraft of three hundred pounds.

I had an Austin 8 but sold it, a decision with which Jill readily agreed if only to be rid once and for all of the arctic draughts she had been obliged to suffer during our courting days. The car was criminally unroadworthy, but it had done its job. We rented a flat at 12 Lower Crescent, off Botanic Avenue in Belfast, at one pound six shillings a week.

In the summer term of 1955 a High Court judge, Charles Sheil, invited me to be his registrar on the forthcoming assizes. Each spring and summer the High Court in a single circuit of assize visited the six counties – County Antrim (at Belfast), County Down (at Downpatrick), County Armagh (at Armagh), County Fermanagh (at Enniskillen), County Tyrone (at Omagh), County Londonderry (at Derry) – and the County Borough of Londonderry (also at Derry) – in that order. Each judge was entitled to appoint a registrar who accompanied him around the circuit and who was paid '£200 Irish' (an honorarium referring to the Irish pound before partition and equivalent to a few pounds less in sterling) – a not insignificant sum in those days and the easiest money I was ever to earn. Expenses for board and lodging were paid by the judges.

The invitation gave me some minor status, and the opportunity of mixing with the provincial legal fraternity. Being a registrar on assize was a valuable experience. There the young barrister saw how the court functioned from the angle both of the Bench and of the Bar. And was paid for it, to boot. I had been selected for this temporary sinecure by the sole Catholic on the High Court Bench of five.

The measured progress of the Queen's justices around the Northern Ireland Circuit, now a thing of the past, was a pleasant diversion enjoyed by all except those on the wrong side of the law. On the morning the assize opened in Derry, the bells of St Columb's Church of Ireland cathedral joyfully greeted the judges as they were received by two trumpeters supplied by the navy, two officers of Londonderry Corporation in uniform, and the city mace-bearer and sword-bearer. Very British. Dinner guests would be the High Sheriff, the County Inspector, Crown counsel, the Crown solicitor, and a few county dignitaries. The conviviality lasted often into the small hours; sleep was of little consequence. My total abstinence at that time worried the judge, who was concerned about the damage that drinking so much orange juice must inevitably cause to my system.

When at Armagh, we would often enjoy the hospitality of the Speaker of the Stormont House of Commons, the kindly and courteous Sir Norman Stronge, at Tynan Abbey. (He and his son James, who sat beside me on the back benches in Stormont when I arrived there, were shot dead by the IRA on 21 January 1981 and Tynan Abbey was burned to the ground.)

It was reassuring for a dutifully deferential young barrister to note that these great men had a less remote and more amiable side to their characters other than the image they presented on the Bench. To share in their off-duty relaxation, to listen to their banter and friendly verbal abuse of each other in my presence, was to be regarded as one of the brotherhood of the Bar, albeit for only two or three weeks. When practising in their courts thereafter, I would know that despite their impatience they were warm human beings at heart.

I was taken out on circuit again by another judge, Arthur Black (Lord Justice Black). Arthur (as he was known by us all) was born in east Belfast, where his father had been headmaster of the national school in Ballymacarrett. He had been a brilliant classical scholar and gained a double first at Sidney Sussex College, Cambridge. He had the intellect and capacity to become distinguished in any academic discipline he might have chosen. By nature a shy, unsophisticated man, something of a recluse, he was always uneasy away from his home at Castlehill Road where he devoted most of his spare time to caring for an invalid sister. He never owned a car and often, when we lived in Cherryvalley Park nearby, I would drive him home at the end of a day's sitting in court.

One day Arthur came into the library looking for me. 'Are you short of money?' he asked.

'Yes, Lord Justice,' I replied.

'Well, how would you like to come out on the circus with me?'

'I'd love to!' Charlie Sheil had this time chosen my friend Robin Rowland as his registrar.

Corick House outside Omagh was the only lodgings that had a piano. After dinner, the judge would ask me to 'play that wee tune', by which I knew he meant the adagio movement from Beethoven's *Pathétique* sonata, a favourite of his. The long hours at the piano in my youth proved to have been worthwhile. However imperfectly I performed I was always flattered to be asked to play.

The first instructions I received on circuit were by way of a dock brief at the Armagh assizes. The accused, an itinerant, was indicted on a charge of robbery with violence to which he pleaded not guilty. He was not represented and had no means of paying for counsel. I had accepted the 'dock brief', as such briefs were known. It would be my first experience before a jury.

At a consultation with the accused in Crumlin Road prison where he was awaiting trial, he insisted he had not tied up the victim of the crime, a little old lady, in her cottage or threatened her with a knife; nor had she handed over £200. As I could see no plausible defence in the face of the evidence that she had had no difficulty in identifying my client at an identification parade, I suggested to him that a plea of guilty might be the better course. He had previous convictions, but the judge might just give him some credit for facing up to the charge and not wasting the court's time. He was adamant, however, that he did not do it.

The only hope I had was the fact that when the lady had entered the room at the police station where a number of suspects were lined up, she had passed my client who was first in the line, gone down to the end, walked back and only then pointed him out. I urged the jury to consider that if she had been sure my client was the guilty man she would have pointed him out immediately she saw him, and that there was therefore a reasonable doubt. The Chief Justice, Lord MacDermott, raised this with the jury in his summing up. My client was acquitted. I turned round to the dock hoping perhaps for some sign of gratitude. He was gone. For the two-day trial I received the princely sum of £4 12s 6d. I am prepared to accept that the successful outcome of that case had little to do with any forensic skill on my part, more with Armagh juries' reputed reluctance to bring in guilty verdicts.

I had a sad court experience at the County Court of Armagh, sitting at the time in Portadown. Turlough (later Lord Justice) O'Donnell and I were contesting a case under the Family Provisions Inheritance Act under which a husband could not totally disinherit his wife. The deceased husband had done just that for reasons I forget, and Turlough's client, the widow, was seeking a share in the estate. When the poor lady had finished her evidence I got up to cross-examine her. I was just about to ask her a second question when she fell out of the witness box, dead, at my feet. The judge, Turlough and I stood looking down at the body. All the judge could think of saying was 'We'll have to adjourn this case', an understatement for all time. When I arrived back at the library later that day the black humour emerged. It was being said that 'McIvor had conducted a deadly cross-examination'.

Despite my slow start, by the mid-1960s I had established a reasonable general practice. As well, I sat on local tribunals under the health and social services legislation and on industrial tribunals concerned with wrongful dismissal and redundancy payments. I also obtained a retainer as junior counsel for the Ulster Transport Authority, which was a steady source of income.

Protestants and Catholics tended to sit at different ends of the Bar Library. And it was the case that solicitors on the whole would brief their co-religionists. But the political tensions that began to emerge in the mid-1960s never spilled over into the Bar Library, which at that time comprised thirty-five Catholics and twenty-two Protestants. There were differing political views to be sure, but members of the Bar kept them to themselves and never allowed them to embitter professional relationships. Most of us were part of that large section of the middle and upper class of Northern Ireland that preferred to leave politics to the politicians.

At the same time there were always a number of Stormont MPs amongst us. In my time at the Bar, before I became an MP, fourteen of my colleagues held Stormont seats – there were ten Unionists (includ-. ing the Attorney-General), one Commonwealth Party MP, two Nationalists and one Liberal.

James McSparran QC, the Nationalist MP for Mourne, whose home-spun style of advocacy was highly effective in court and before a jury, was a good man of very high principles who respected the opinions of his brethren – barristers of the Unionist persuasion – where they differed from his own. A dark, handsome, warmhearted and sociable man, seldom without a red rose in his lapel, he was greatly respected by us all. His wholesome, calming influence in the Bar Library was a considerable factor in closing out or down any tension within it. I was agreeably surprised and encouraged when he confided to me during the 1969 O'Neill elections that he had done me no harm in Andersonstown – the Catholic sector of the Larkfield constituency for which I was fighting on the O'Neill Unionist ticket – implying that he had helped me behind the scenes.

The Bar was a world apart. But in the mid-1960s most of us were genuinely alarmed at events outside. For forty years we had been governed by a 'Protestant parliament for a Protestant people', a situation that was rationalised and justified by the majority in terms of simple democracy. The result, however, was the sterile politics of one-party rule by the Unionist Party (itself closely linked with the Orange Order) which completely alienated the Catholics who regarded themselves as second-class citizens, their inferior civil status being reinforced by discrimination in local government. The two distinct communities were growing farther apart, and it was not until Terence O'Neill became prime minister in 1963 that there was any recognition on the part of Protestant opinion of the potentially explosive situation and the urgency of reform. The brief history of Northern Ireland, despite remarkable progress in the economic field, was not one of which I was proud. There had been nearly fifty years of Protestant rule based on widespread and indefensible discrimination. Yet Protestants, however erroneously, regarded this as being a consequence of Catholic unwillingness to participate, rather than of active exclusion by the majority. In fact it was a mixture of both. And in a sense, because discrimination became institutionalised within the state, because Protestants grew up in Protestant areas, went to Protestant schools and worked in Protestant factories, it was lack of direct contact with Catholics that tended to secure mutual antagonism and fear, rather than overt physical conflict penetrating all of society. The communities were separate, and most working-class Protestants drew their political attitudes from their culture – in the absence of anything more than fleeting contact with their Catholic neighbours. Protestants and Catholics have paid dearly over nearly three decades for this separate development and segregation. It has for each generation been the tragic inheritance of history.

The status of Catholics in the Unionist scheme of things was to be publicly underlined in June 1968 when the Nationalist MP Austin Currie (the youngest MP ever returned to Stormont) squatted as a protest in 9 Kinnaird Place in Caledon, County Tyrone. The house had been let to a single nineteen-year-old Protestant woman at a time when there were 269 applicants on the local housing list, the vast majority of them Catholics with families. Currie attracted widespread television and media coverage for his action.

A most blatant act of discrimination nearer home – in the Bar Library itself – was equally disturbing. The death of Sam Porter in 1957 left a vacancy on the High Court Bench which comprised five judges. The leading silk, Cyril Nicholson QC, an obvious choice for the vacancy, happened to be a Catholic. Unquestionably qualified for preferment, his claim to the vacancy would, I know, have had the wholehearted support of members of the Bar. But there was already a Catholic on the High Court Bench: Charles Sheil. It would have been inconvenient for the political establishment when Brookeborough was prime minister to have had two Catholic High Court judges out of five. A Protestant silk was appointed.

When in 1966 I received the telephone call asking me if I would allow my name to go forward as a Unionist candidate for North Armagh as the sitting MP was thought to be about to retire, I decided to throw my hat in the ring. I became a member of the Unionist Party and shortly afterwards chairman of the Bloomfield Unionist Association. I did not win the nomination for North Armagh, not surprisingly as I had not canvassed any delegates, never mind attended the nomination meeting. The sitting MP, who was not for retiring, had it all sewn up, although I was told that I did receive a respectable number of votes from delegates in the farming community.

Some well-meaning friends at the time, siren voices, accosted me with a friendly pat on the back, suggesting I was the very man for the job, the man who might help to break the mould and clear out the Augean stables up at Stormont – no one better, good luck! The assailants would then settle down behind a substantial pile of briefs on their desk in the library or return to some prosperous business in town, leaving me at once flattered and uneasy, and suddenly less than courageous.

One of the features of the thirty years of the Troubles has been how the middle class in Northern Ireland has, for the most part, kept its collective head down and refused to become involved, preferring to be seen as apolitical and neutral. They could afford to be aloof. The North's well-to-do have largely managed to come through unscathed. There have been notable exceptions, some paying with their lives. There are those, for example, who have been labelled by the IRA as 'part of the British war machine' – judges, magistrates, civil servants, and businessmen supplying or thought to be supplying the security forces. William Staunton, Rory Conaghan, Martin McBirney, William Doyle and Maurice Gibson – these friends and colleagues of mine at the Bar were murdered by the IRA because they came within that category. The generality of the middle and upper classes, however, have managed – apart from the unavoidable irritants such as traffic jams, roadblocks or office chaos after bombs or bomb alerts – to come through undamaged and with few casualties. The culture was one of aloofness, of being 'above it all', of distancing themselves from two sets of proletarian tribes fighting out an atavistic war – 'the apolitical vision'.

To be fair, this is not an unusual or surprising human reaction in troubled times. It is said that citizens living on the outskirts of pre-revolutionary Paris would have been totally unaware of the fall of the

Bastille. Life went on normally, as it often does in the midst of social upheaval.

If I was waylaid by those encouraging me to seek a larger good than that of a self-serving barrister, I had no one but myself to blame. But wiser heads were shaking: 'What does a decent fellow like McIvor want to get mixed up in politics for?' One of those heads was my cautious father's. (He and my mother were living with us in Cherryvalley Park, where they spent the rest of their lives after my father's retirement in 1962. By this time, also, our three children, Jonathan, Timothy and Jane, had all been born.) In any event, in 1968 when Brian McConnell (now Lord McConnell of Lisburn), then minister of home affairs at Stormont, resigned his office to become a National Insurance Commissioner, a window of opportunity suddenly opened for me. He represented the large constituency of South Antrim which comprised the area running roughly from the King's Hall at Balmoral to Aghalee on the shores of Lough Neagh, and from the Hannahstown Road above west Belfast across to Finaghy and Dunmurry.

Bob Armour, the general manager of the Commercial Union Assurance Company, which regularly gave me briefs, agreed to act as my agent in the by-election for the seat. Bob was a shrewd, resourceful and diplomatic election agent. I have everything to thank him for in the support he gave me, which ultimately led to a seat in Stormont. He knew the constituency inside out. Having in the past played hockey for Lisnagarvey, and cricket at a high level, he had many influential friends in the constituency.

September 1968 was a month of beautiful weather. Bob, Jill and I worked the huge constituency in unbroken sunshine. There were fifteen Unionist candidates for the nomination, one of whom was a barrister colleague, Richard Ferguson, whom we would meet on occasion coming down the lane from the home of a delegate we were going up to canvass. He was usually ahead of us.

My not being a member of the Orange Order was a problem for us. As there had not been an election in this constituency for many years, the list of Orange delegates was out of date and in the process of being revised. We could never be sure whether the list we had was correct, whether it needed adding to or deleting from. Unionist headquarters tried to help, but it was unnerving to see deleted from the daily revisions names of people on whom we had lavished time and effort; meanwhile there were ever new ones to be tackled. Ferguson, an Orangeman, had the advantage.

I never had any desire to join the Orange Order. The survival of the Protestant faith, certainly my personal brand of Protestantism, did not require bolstering or defending in this way. But especially I knew I would not feel comfortable with the shibboleths, oaths and declarations, or the flags and emblems that others thought necessary in order to demonstrate where they stood in religion and politics. Moreover, the possibility of having to live in a state suppressed by a callous and ruthless Catholic theocracy did not seem to me, then, a likely scenario – nor, indeed, does it now. I was not at the time asked to join the order as a condition of being permitted to seek election to Stormont as a Unionist MP. For this I was, and am, grateful.

I remember one glorious evening canvassing the vote of a farmer building a hayrick. Without stopping what he was doing, over his shoulder he asked Bob whether I could 'handle that fella Gerry Fitt'. Bob assured him that I could – no problem. On many occasions Gerry had represented his constituents before local tribunals I was chairing under the health and social services legislation. I had come to know and enjoy his disarming good humour and breezy manner. Who should fear what he knows so well?

Another delegate informed me, apparently by way of approval, 'Mr McIvor, I'll not loss no sleep if you get in.' A spirited discussion about Northern Ireland politics in the living room of one delegate in Lisburn was suddenly stopped in its tracks by a shrill voice from the corner of the room: 'Come on, give us a wee kiss then!' I at least had the support of the budgie.

The night of the selection arrived – a dark September evening, pouring with rain. The selection was held in the Orange Hall in Lisburn, at the corner of Wallace Avenue and Railway Street. The candidates duly made their presentations to the 180 delegates. Richard Ferguson's Orange credentials were impeccable. It soon became clear, after the eliminations, that it was between the two of us. I lost the nomination by four votes.

Outside, under a sickly green fluorescent light, Bob's face had a deathlike pallor. 'Basil,' he said simply and sadly, 'we're bate.' It was a bitter pill. Back home my father was relieved. My mother, who had something more aggressive in her character, which I shared, felt my disappointment keenly. I saw a tear slowly trickle down the cheek of our thirteen-year-old, Jonathan.

In the ensuing by-election, Dick Ferguson was duly elected MP for South Antrim. Shortly afterwards he left the Orange Order, and in February 1970 he resigned as MP for health reasons, resuming his practice at the Northern Ireland Bar. (This he left in 1984 to pursue his profession at the English Bar, where he has since become a high-profile trial lawyer.)

As it turned out, this exercise gave me a head start when it came to the choice of a Unionist candidate for the constituency of Larkfield a few months later.

3

POISONED CHALICE

T HE PREMIERSHIP OF TERENCE O'NEILL from 1963 to 1969 marked a defining break with the past. Although with his air of *amour propre* he tended to remain remote from ordinary people, he departed from the 'not an inch' mentality of previous prime ministers and made a commitment to improve community relations the main plank in his platform. At the same time a new generation of Catholic leaders was emerging, along with a growing Catholic middle class which was turning to political action after the failure of the IRA's fifties campaign. Shortly after O'Neill's meeting in January 1965 with Sean Lemass, the Irish taoiseach (the first such meeting since the Northern Ireland state was founded), Eddie McAteer, Nationalist MP for Foyle, accepted the role of official opposition leader at Stormont –

before that, the Nationalist Party had been the main vehicle of anti-partition policies. McAteer consistently argued at Stormont that much trouble might have been avoided if Unionists had offered concessions at that period.

Yet by 1968, Protestant reaction to reform moves was already manifest. It was led by Ian Paisley and to a lesser extent by Harry West, Bill Craig and William Morgan. As Brian Faulkner pointed out in his *Memoirs of a Statesman* (although he himself at the time had still to be converted to the liberal cause):

> Too much publicity about our wish to change only fed the fears which Ian Paisley was beginning to exploit: fears that better North/South relations might undermine Ulster's position as part of the United Kingdom; fears that the South was only trying to find a new way of effecting its claim on our territory; fears aroused by the massive republican celebrations of the fiftieth anniversary of the 1916 Uprising and the accompanying riots; and fears that the ecumenical movement was in Northern Ireland designed to reduce opposition to a takeover by the Catholic Irish Republic.

The objectives of the Northern Ireland Civil Rights Association (NICRA) founded in 1967 were legitimate demands which Protestants might have conceded: a points system to ensure a fair allocation of housing; legislation against discrimination in local government employment; the redrawing of electoral boundaries by an independent commission to ensure fair representation; universal adult suffrage in local government elections; repeal of the Special Powers Act; and disbandment of the B Specials.

But there was a restricting factor, which was the violent reaction to the marches – especially in Derry on 5 October 1968 when the police baton-charged a civil rights march resulting in widespread rioting, and later at the 'battle of Burntollet Bridge' on 4 January 1969, when police stood by as loyalist extremists ambushed and stoned a march out of Claudy. It soon emerged that a large number of these Protestants were off-duty B Specials. This violence, with march and countermarch, marked the start of major civil strife, and politically drove moderate Catholic and Protestant opinion to their respective corners. Among the Catholic population, despite efforts of nonviolent NICRA leaders, it was to mean the imminent reinsurgence of the IRA, who latched easily onto legitimate grievances. To the Protestants it implied a fundamental threat. What began as a civil rights movement erupted into sectarian conflict between the aggrieved minority and the apprehensive majority and quickly merged into a conflict not over questions of social justice and reform within Northern Ireland, but over the very issue of the state itself.

In fact O'Neill managed to get cabinet approval for a five-point programme of reforms, which he announced in November 1968. They were: (1) a fair allocation of housing based on a points system; (2) appointment of an 'ombudsman' to investigate grievances; (3) replacement of Londonderry Corporation by a broadly based Development Commission; (4) abolition of the company vote in local elections, and general reform and modernisation of local government ('one man, one vote' was introduced for local elections the following April); and (5) a review of the Special Powers Act (clauses conflicting with the UK's international obligations were to be removed).

It was in the context of these political developments that when O'Neill called a snap general election in February 1969 I sought the Unionist nomination for the newly created Larkfield seat which had replaced one of the recently abolished Queen's University seats. The constituency took in the densely populated areas of Finaghy, Dunmurry and Malone (mainly Protestant), Andersonstown (Catholic) and Suffolk (mainly Protestant at that time) with an electorate of 20,774. The political landscape was daunting for someone who had hitherto led a peaceful, relatively uncomplicated life in a close family setting.

My motives were mixed. Ambition, restlessness, the pressing call by Terence O'Neill for the Unionist Party to support him in creating a more acceptable Northern Ireland, together with an intrinsic sense of public duty which has plagued me throughout my life, all played their part in my decision to enter the maelstrom of political life as a Stormont member of parliament.

The new Larkfield seat had been carved out of the former South Antrim constituency and I was already well-known to the delegates of the Unionist Association. This time there was no canvassing and the delegates of necessity made a quick decision. On securing the Unionist nomination I received a letter from Jack Sayers, the editor of the *Belfast Telegraph*, that was encouraging, though unnerving in its over-estimation of my potential as a politician:

February 11, 1969

Dear Basil McIvor

I am delighted to know that you are to be the candidate in Larkfield – and that your association wants you to support the PM. May you be at the head of the poll and have a long and successful career in politics. I am quite sure that you are the kind of man who will help to redeem the party – how much it needs it! Please don't reply.

Good Fortune,

Jack Sayers

The general election campaign took place in bitterly cold weather. Canvassing in the February snow led Ian Paisley, who was contesting Terence O'Neill's Bannside seat, to observe with characteristic mordant wit: 'Nobody but a snowman would call an election at this time of the year. But you know what happens to a snowman when the heat's on!'

O'Neill won his seat with a majority of only 1,414, out of an electorate of 20,685 with a poll of 78.7 per cent. His poor showing in the poll was evidence of unmistakable resentment of his insistence that this 'crossroads election' was the last chance for Ulster people to vote for sensible, reformist policies that would ensure Northern Ireland's continued membership of the UK.

Bob Armour, my election agent, was a tower of strength. We canvassed diligently throughout my densely populated constituency with the assistance of my director of communications, the brilliant, energetic and always cheerful Harry Calvert, at the time a senior lecturer in the Law Faculty at Queen's University. Harry organised a team of students from Queen's University to canvass for me and would himself proclaim to the constituents of Larkfield, by loud-hailer from a hired car, the merits of the candidate. Some of my colleagues from the Bar were also very generous with their time on my behalf, tirelessly tramping the streets. And I shall always be grateful to Arthur Jenkins and his wife Muriel, whose flat at Suffolk was an oasis where we were fed and watered when we gathered to rest up and take stock.

There was another home into which we were welcomed during canvassing. When the door of the semi-detached house was opened to us on our first visit, I looked past the lady of the house into the living room and noticed on top of the TV set a large photograph of the Queen in her Garter robes and the Duke of Edinburgh in the uniform of an Admiral of the Fleet. This was most reassuring, never mind the surprise that Her Majesty could count on some loyal subjects in Catholic Andersonstown. The photographs looked very new and were clearly prominently placed so that no one entering the room could possibly avoid noticing them. Bob and I paid several visits to this house during the campaign and were always encouraged to believe that the Union was secure there anyway. On election day I happened to be speaking to a gathering outside a nearby polling station, restating my conviction that the welfare of Ulster was best secured by its remaining part of the United Kingdom and that I wholeheartedly supported the policies of Captain O'Neill, where equal justice for all was the sole end of the use of public power. I believed the task of government to be to guarantee jobs, houses and adequate living conditions for all regardless of class and creed, and that despite everything it was possible to create in Ulster a just, prosperous and harmonious society. If elected, I would pursue these aims with all my power. I was convinced that the vast majority of the people of Ulster wished to create such a society, but that it could only be achieved 'if the people as a whole expressed their desire for it'.

When I had finished, our hostess of a few days ago came out of the crowd and approached me in apparent distress. She said she had taken two pounds belonging to her husband from the mantelpiece in her living room without his knowledge, and that as he was a hard and violent man (indeed in the employ of one of HM's prisons) she feared for her safety when he arrived home for his tea and the missing notes had not been replaced. Just at the moment she had not the cash to do so – could I possibly lend her two pounds? Being taken completely by surprise and feeling the pressure of the occasion with the crowd standing round having listened to me very civilly, I slowly put my right hand into my pocket to search for the money. Simultaneously I felt a vicelike grip on my arm and Bob's whisper through clenched teeth: 'Don't do it, it's a trap!' And on looking around I saw those who would undoubtedly be prepared to testify that they had seen the Unionist candidate attempting to bribe the electorate. That could well have spelt the end of my interest in the O'Neill election. Good for Bob!

The count for Larkfield took place in the old Grand Jury room in the Crumlin Road courthouse. We were confident that we had done well. On the day before the election, when, footsore and weary, we gathered to assess the situation, Harry Calvert put the odds on me in a robustly indelicate way by prophesying that nothing could stop me winning unless, between then and the end of voting the next day, I were to be discovered raping a nun in Royal Avenue – in broad daylight. Nevertheless, I shall never forget the sickening anxiety I felt in that room as the voting papers tumbled out of the boxes.

It soon became clear that I was receiving a substantial vote. There were three other candidates – Tom Sherry (National Democratic Party), Tom Magee (Northern Ireland Labour Party) and Gerry O'Hare (Republican Labour Party); 68.3 per cent of the electorate voted and my majority, as a Unionist, was 6,115. The electorate of the new Stormont seat of Larkfield, which was half and half Protestant and Catholic, had spoken in my favour and we were entitled to sit for a while on cloud nine. For the moment the pre-election commitments to be honoured and the implications of a future high public profile, which would change our lives, were put to the back of our minds. We had made it!

Shortly afterwards, I was entering the Royal Courts of Justice behind the tall figure of the Lord Chief Justice, Lord MacDermott, when he stopped, obviously wishing to speak, and waited for me to catch up. I assumed that he was about to congratulate me and cheerfully stood my ground. How mistaken I was. He bluntly accused me of having become a Unionist MP as a means of 'getting a job' – meaning, in effect, seeking preferment to the Bench. It was well known that some members of the Bar down the years had used Stormont as a staging post for the Bench. For some of these the Bench would probably have been out of their reach otherwise. Others would have arrived there in any event on merit, but nevertheless furnished themselves with a Unionist seat at Stormont just to be on the safe side. Several, I knew, had tried to secure a Unionist seat and failed.

Unprepared for this unexpected rebuke I was lost for an immediate appropriate response and at a loss to understand why I should have to justify my decision to him. I was aware that in his early days at the Bar His Lordship had been elected as a Unionist MP for the Queen's University constituency which led to him later becoming attorney-general. So I might have replied, if I had had the courage, that active support for Terence O'Neill's increasingly despairing crusade for reform of the notorious discriminatory administration of the Unionist establishment, of which he had once been part, was justification enough. Too late – the moment had gone. In any event, Unionist patronage in the legal profession was to become a thing of the past with, amongst other evidence, the report of the Cameron Commission of Inquiry which Terence O'Neill had set up in January 1969.

Realistically it would have taken someone of unusual capacity to carry on a serious practice at the Bar at the same time as being totally involved in the politics of an increasingly unstable and manifestly moribund system of government, and at a time when the community was daily experiencing ever higher peaks of violence. It was important to me not to be viewed as an amateur who had strayed into politics with only half his mind on the game. I had chosen to pursue my firm conviction that political change was needed if the state of Northern Ireland was to survive. The system rested on an insecure foundation of appealing to one sector of the population at the expense of the other. The minority needed a sensible and positive response to the increasing demands for change.

It was now abundantly clear that, so far as my future at the Bar was concerned, I would be struck off the list of hopefuls. The option of playing for safety had gone. I had joined the ranks of the risk takers. My heart sank. Had my career taken a serious misdirection? I was no longer one of the pack.

4

THE BEGINNING OF THE END

> Our little systems have their day;
> They have their day and cease to be . . .
> ALFRED, LORD TENNYSON, *In Memoriam*

THE BRITISH GOVERNMENT SPARED NO EXPENSE in 1928 in its gift of the building that was to house the legislature and executive of the parliament of Northern Ireland. This splendid structure, built on a grand scale in Greek classical style, was a symbol of Northern Ireland's identity, an expression of Northern Ireland's determination to have its own parliament albeit subordinate to Westminster – but an emphatic statement of its own importance.

And despite the building's splendid outward appearance the visitor is not disappointed when entering the grand central hall lined with Roman marble columns, its ceiling of intricate designs picked out in glowing blue, red and gold, the marble floor repeating the geometry of the ceiling.

I had never seen any of this splendour before the day in February 1969 that I was escorted to the Clerk's Table in the Commons debating chamber to sign in as the newly elected MP for the constituency of Larkfield at the salary of £2,500 a year together with £300 secretarial expenses and travel expenses to and from my constituency to Stormont. After the bruising experience of getting there I could not but be mightily impressed by all this grandeur, made available by the Mother of Parliaments across in Britain, and for such a tiny piece of territory. It looked as if the struggle to get there was all worthwhile. What a splendid place in which to legislate for the welfare of 1.5 million souls.

Here I was, sitting on the green benches in the debating chamber at Stormont, one of fifty-two unionist MPs of differing unionist complexions – a very fragmented lot. At one end of the spectrum was Johnny McQuade, one of the best-known personalities on the Protestant Shankill Road in Belfast. He was a decent man, earnestly and often fiercely loyalist, an ex-docker, ex-soldier and ex-boxer who, when later the Nothern Ireland Assembly was prorogued in May 1974, refused to take his salary and donated it to a holiday fund for old people. (At the same end of the political spectrum, Ian Paisley did not make his appearance until April 1970 when he won a by-election in Bannside, County Antrim, O'Neill's former seat.) At the other end of the spectrum were the liberal Unionist MPs, including Anne Dickson (the only woman MP), Robin Bailie and myself and the languidly independent pro-O'Neill Unionist Tom Caldwell.

For the first time I was to come into contact with the new, younger brand of politicians who the following year were to found the Social Democratic and Labour Party (SDLP) – John Hume, Ivan Cooper, Paddy O'Hanlon, Austin Currie, the older Gerry Fitt (Republican Labour Party) and the occasionally irreverent Paddy Devlin, a member of the Northern Ireland Labour Party. When the SDLP was founded it was as a radical left-of-centre party that would seek civil rights for all and just distribution of wealth. They would work towards their eventual goal of a united Ireland through improving friendship and understanding between North and South. (Fitt was to break with the SDLP mainly because it was becoming less socialist and 'more green nationalist'. Devlin was expelled in 1977 complaining that the party was reducing the socialist content of its policy.)

Any delusions of grandeur I might have had when I first entered Stormont were fairly quickly dispelled. Some unionists in this *sanctum sanctorum* of Unionist power and domination went well ahead on points when it came to the disruption of the proceedings from time to time. The boorish excesses and saloon-bar tendencies of these members were in stark contrast to the opposition which, when they were not boycotting the proceedings, would prefer to sit on the floor of the chamber singing 'We shall not be moved'. This was not, I thought, in the same category as the outrageous violence of some of 'Her Majesty's most loyal subjects' which I was shortly to witness.

I had little opportunity to play myself in as a new boy. I went straight into the fray, spending most of my time outside supporting Terence O'Neill's fight for his political life. He had already been badly damaged by the resignation from the cabinet of his minister of commerce, Brian Faulkner, and William Morgan, his minister of health. Both disagreed with O'Neill's decision to set up the three-man Cameron Commission of Inquiry to trace the causes of violence in the community since October 1968, and to identify those bodies responsible for contributing to the unrest.

Although O'Neill's leadership had been confirmed by the Unionist Parliamentary Party after the election of February 1969, his was no more than a confused and Pyrrhic victory. Twenty-three MPs voted for the reform proposals based on the findings of the Cameron Commission; Brian Faulkner was amongst those who voted against. The election, with its division of pro- and anti-O'Neill candidates, left a legacy of bitterness throughout Unionism at a time when the pressure for change from the civil rights movement was intensifying. O'Neill had taken the gamble of endorsing pro-O'Neill candidates who, in many cases, were opposing the official nominees of the local Unionist associations – hence the bitterness. He had no power base from which to launch his series of reforms.

I was a zealous supporter of his new deal for Northern Ireland but did not find him an easy leader. I was impressed with the message but not with the messenger. His patrician, somewhat languid air was not the best medium for the herculean task of advancing the need for social reform and bringing in from the cold the alienated Catholic one-third of the community. But it was he and he alone who broke the mould. History will remember him kindly as the politician who pointed Northern Ireland to higher ground and a better way. He created opportunities for people like myself to become involved in government at the highest level.

But O'Neill lacked the common touch. He was a man of deep and potent reforming convictions, but what came across was his uncomfortableness at his own lack of ease with himself. He found it difficult to communicate warmth and friendliness – although those who knew him well believed he possessed both these qualities. It would require a more heroic figure to allay the Protestant fears that fuelled what has been termed the siege mentality. I found him distant and uninspiring. I would not, I confess, have felt like dying in a ditch for him.

I remember well one revealing incident, which occurred when he came to tour Andersonstown with me before the election. An over-enthusiastic lady who was endeavouring to reach him through the crowd to shake his hand fell off a low ramp, about two feet high, outside the supermarket known as the Busy Bee. Some of us paused to help her to her feet. O'Neill, who had seen the incident, pushed us on regardless, leaving the unfortunate lady to pick herself up. It was an occasion when he could have done himself some good by stopping to make sure the poor lady had come to no harm. He did not possess the chemistry for that sort of response. Nor did he always express himself well. I was embarrassed when, with naïve condescension, he suggested in the course of a radio interview that if Catholics were given decent housing they would begin to live like Protestants. We held our breath for what was coming next.

I came to dread meetings at Unionist Party headquarters in Glengall Street, where O'Neill would courageously and stubbornly advocate the need for reform. As prime minister and leader of the Unionist Party he might reasonably have expected solid support from the party machine.

But this was not forthcoming. Northern Ireland was being virtually run from Glengall Street, the powerhouse of the party machine, not from Stormont. The party apparatchiks were not listening to moderate opinion. We knew that the secretary was holding Saturday-morning sessions to which only right-wing elements would be invited, to enable him to find out how they were reacting to the volatile and changing political scene.

To get the message of the party across more effectively and to improve its image throughout the UK and abroad it was decided to establish a public relations department at Glengall Street. Trevor Hanna, a professional journalist with considerable local and national experience, was approached to set it up and was offered a contract as its director. He found, however, that he was being frustrated in the carrying out of the job he was hired to do. A battle over reform was raging between party HQ and the Government Information Service at Stormont Castle, which supported the liberal side. Speeches and other publicity material prepared by the Government Information Service and sent to Glengall Street for clearance were being censored and altered where they appeared too liberal. Trevor Hanna was quickly to realise that the Glengall Street clique was a Trojan Horse. Instead of supporting O'Neill by showing the right-wing element in the party the door, this clique was pandering to it and becoming a vehicle for dissenting views. Terence O'Neill was being undermined by his own party machine. Trevor Hanna refused to allow the department he headed to be used as a platform for diehard rhetoric. Thwarted by the very people who had appointed him, he showed his frustration by declining to renew his contract. He walked out after twelve months to return to the freedom of the press.

Unfortunately, O'Neill's dreary, measured and somewhat plaintive manner of delivery was hardly likely to fire his supporters, never mind change the views of his opponents. The hardliners who at these awful Glengall Street meetings invariably gave him a very hard time insisted that he was undermining and destroying the state. The battle for the hearts and minds of the Unionist Party was not going to be won there. In the wider community there was a large moderate but tacit body of support for him, both Protestant and Catholic. If only this middle-ground unionist support had had the courage actively to back him at that crucial time, we might not have had to endure the social upheaval and dreadful tragedies that were to follow and continue for nearly three decades. At a time of great moral crisis the vast majority of the moderate middle and upper classes maintained their neutrality. In the midst of uncertainty it was impossible to secure the silent majority in the struggle against the populism of an Ian Paisley, whose apocalyptic rhetoric exploited genuine doubts and fears of many unionists on the threat of Rome and the threat to the Union. As my good friend Tom Wilson, an Ulsterman from Ballynure in County Antrim, and one-time Adam Smith Professor of Political Economy at the University of Glasgow, writes in his book *Ulster: Conflict and Consent*: 'No one can, indeed, deny that, in times of stress and uncertainty in Ulster or anywhere else, a firm belief of some kind can provide assurance and support.' After so long in power, Unionists would not willingly slay the dragons of their own imagination.

In these circumstances the moderate voice of compromise was not easily heard. We were unlikely to get many people to drop what they were doing and come forward in support. Under threat from the loyalist paramilitaries – who were attempting to destabilise O'Neill and end the reform programme by means of attacks on Belfast's main source of water supply – and fatally undermined by the resignation of hardliners from his cabinet, Terence O'Neill resigned on 28 April 1969 – two months after the election. On television that night he said:

> I have tried to break the chains of ancient hatreds. I have been unable to realise during my period in office all that I sought to achieve. Whether now it can be achieved in my lifetime I do not know. But one day these will be and must be achieved.

Most of his reforms were ultimately carried despite the resistance of his erstwhile enemies. He has earned a place in history for changing the politics of Northern Ireland for the better.

James Chichester-Clark (affectionately known as Chi-Chi) had resigned as minister of agriculture five days previously, following speculation that he might become premier if O'Neill went. The ostensible reason for Chi-Chi's departure was the timing of the 'one man, one vote' reform, although he said he was not against the principle. But his resignation put the final nail in O'Neill's coffin.

On 1 May 1969, Chichester-Clark was elected leader of the Ulster Unionist Party by seventeen votes to sixteen over Brian Faulkner. On reflection I regret not having given Brian Faulkner my vote. I have no doubt that this was a mistake – but from my point of view understandable, for had not Brian distanced himself from Terence O'Neill's reforms? As minister of commerce he had absented himself to the United States, albeit seeking investment in Northern Ireland, when the going was getting very rough for O'Neill back home. I saw him as a hardliner. I believe now that I misjudged him then. He was essentially a fair-minded, even-handed politician of great integrity, who would never have countenanced discrimination in any form. He happened also to be ambitious. O'Neill was in his way. The objections he may have had to O'Neill's reforming policies were simply in the course of distancing himself from a lame duck whom he hoped to replace some day.

I have often since wondered whether events would have taken a different course had my vote been for Faulkner. We liberals had difficulty in identifying where he stood in the Unionist spectrum. The *Irish Times* had categorised him as 'the soft-hardliner'. With hindsight I am now sure he would have responded more readily to insistent demands for reform from a disaffected large minority, and got away with it as a much abler politician. James Chichester-Clark, an imposing figure, had kept a low profile. He looked as if he might be more forceful in handling the increasingly complex affairs of Northern Ireland. But he had no real track record upon which one could judge his leadership qualities. *The Times* got it wrong, too. 'Chichester-Clark, the safer choice,' it said.

Only a few days before O'Neill's resignation, the Parliamentary Commissioner Bill, introduced on 23 April 1969, had given me a useful occasion for my maiden speech. The proposed legislation would establish a Parliamentary Commissioner for Administration (an ombudsman), who would be independent of the government and would investigate 'administrative action taken on behalf of the Crown for Her Majesty's Government in Northern Ireland' (it was an office to which my wife Jill was to be appointed twenty-five years later).

Two privileges attached to maiden speeches. First, the new member was generally called upon, by courtesy, in preference to other members rising at the same time. Second, the member was allowed to speak uninterrupted, enjoying the undivided attention of the House. The downside was that no backbencher was permitted to read from a speech. It was a daunting experience in an alien environment.

I said that the new constituency of Larkfield – which had never before been heard of in the House – had spoken with a new voice. It was a microcosm of Ulster. The politics of its electors ranged from extreme radical to ultra-conservative. I had been elected mainly on a platform of equal citizenship for all individuals of whatever class or creed, a platform that sought to make equality and justice the sole end of the use of public power. Too many people revered the symbols but ignored the duties and responsibilities of British citizenship. I therefore welcomed the opportunity of making my maiden speech on the first reforming measure of that parliament, which would extend justice to the ordinary man and woman when confronted with government maladministration. Members, as guardians of the interests of the citizen, needed a heavier weapon than merely the right to ask questions in the House and the corridors outside. I welcomed the opportunity the Bill offered to vindicate those local authorities whose administration was perfectly proper but who were subjected to a continuous stream of accusations. Until wrongs were righted and false charges were exposed, we would never be free from the sense of grievance that had spread throughout society. I argued that redress of grievances was a fundamental of British justice. It was not merely that we had to pay for the British connection: fair play was the very reason for maintaining it. After half a century of insecurity, mistrust and fear it was time we got round to accepting what membership of the Union entailed.

I knew that whilst many decent Unionists had no difficulty in subscribing to these convictions, they nevertheless saw them as threatening the abandonment of the state to its enemies. Realistically I did not expect widespread support outside the House for views of this kind.

Indeed, I quickly ran into trouble. Early on, a Unionist Party meeting in the Protestant end of my constituency at Dunmurry reminded me of the enemy without and within. The guest speaker was a member of the cabinet. When I entered the hall with him, most of the audience stood up and clapped us to the platform. Ominously, in two rows at the back and two at the front the people kept their seats. Even more portentous, we noticed that they had brought bibles, upon which some were sitting. A rising chorus of 'traitor' and 'Papish-lover' came from these two rows. As soon as there was a lull, the chairman of my constituency, William Fitch (a young accountant and a member of a Christian businessmen's group) rapped the table, called for attention and suggested that we all stand for a moment of prayer before proceeding. Everyone rose to their feet including the front and back two rows. The prayer asked for, amongst other things, God's presence and blessing on the meeting, and committed our deliberations to Him. Fitch had spiked their guns and there was no further trouble. The meeting passed off in peace, if not in love and harmony. The power of prayer was never more evident.

As serious rioting deteriorated into open sectarian conflict in July and August 1969, a moderate MP like myself became virtually an irrelevance. Protestant fears that the very existence of Northern Ireland was under threat were intensifying as one day of violence followed another. The Stormont government was pushed increasingly on to the back foot. What message of hope for the future could I bring my constituents at the numerous meetings where I was called upon to explain the latest outrage? As a representative of the ruling party I was in an extremely uncomfortable position. On one occasion, along with Father Desmond Wilson, I visited schoolchildren victims of the CS gas used to quell riots in Andersonstown. I felt totally inadequate as all I could offer was sympathy. Desmond Wilson subsequently expressed views which many, including myself, felt were sympathetic to the Sinn Féin/IRA position. I remembered Yeats's poem 'The Second Coming':

> Things fall apart; the centre cannot hold;
> Mere anarchy is loosed upon the world,
> The blood-dimmed tide is loosed, and everywhere
> The ceremony of innocence is drowned;

The best lack all conviction, while the worst
Are full of passionate intensity.

Each morning I dreaded the sound of the first bus (the number 76) from
the city centre as it turned the corner into Cherryvalley Park and, with a
deep-throated roar, climbed the hill past our house, announcing the
beginning of yet another day of doubt, confusion, and uncertainty.

The month of August 1969 saw some of the worst violence so far in
Belfast and Derry. In Derry the Battle of the Bogside, triggered when
the Apprentice Boys paraded past the Catholic Bogside area, left a
thousand RUC officers exhausted after a night's violence. The Catholics
had defended their corner in the Bogside after the police entered it on
14 August with armoured vehicles and water cannon. The rioters threw
stones and petrol bombs from behind barricades, and the police
responded with CS gas.

That month we took a holiday away from it all on the River
Shannon. Hiring a cabin cruiser at Carrick-on-Shannon, we went
down as far as Killaloe near Limerick. It was a glorious trip and did
much to recharge batteries. At Killaloe, however, we were forcibly
reminded of what was happening back in the 'black North' when on
13 August we heard on the radio the voice of the taoiseach, Jack
Lynch, making his 'we will not stand idly by' broadcast in which he
announced that Irish army field hospitals would be set up near the
border in the expectation of a wholesale exodus from the North by
Catholic refugees. He said:

It is clear now that the present situation cannot be allowed to
continue. It is evident that the Stormont government is no longer
in control of the situation. Indeed the present situation is the
inevitable outcome of the policies pursued for decades by successive Stormont governments. It is clear also that the Irish government can no longer stand by and see innocent people injured and
perhaps worse.

The next day I decided to turn the boat round and head back north,
anxious not to be offside if parliament should be recalled. On the way
back a telegram reached me from the Speaker saying that 'IN THE

PUBLIC INTEREST' parliament would meet earlier than scheduled 'ON THURSDAY THE FOURTEENTH DAY OF AUGUST 1969'. There was no possibility of getting back in time.

The journey north was not without incident. In Lough Ree, my mind was obviously on other things, and the cruiser violently struck a submerged rock when passing too close to a buoy. Jill had been about to light the gas oven below. She came up on deck to see what had happened, having left the gas turned on. On returning below she struck another match, and ignited the accumulated gas causing an explosion that singed her eyebrows and hair, but fortunately caused no more serious injury.

It was with a heavy heart that I made my way back into the thick of things. By the time we got back home the 3rd Battalion, Light Infantry, had taken up duty in Andersonstown, where a curfew had been put in position. I had to deal with numerous complaints that young people were unable, because of the curfew, to attend night classes in the centre of Belfast. A short time later a motorcyclist arrived at my home to deliver my copy of the Cameron Report.

On 12 September the Cameron Commission officially published its report to the effect that since 5 October 1968 there had been a failure of leadership on all sides, and that the Stormont government had been 'hidebound' and 'complacent'. Specifically, as noted by W.D. Flackes and Sydney Elliott (*Northern Ireland: A Political Directory 1968–1993*), the report found a 'rising sense of continuing injustice and grievance among large sections of the Catholic population, particularly because of the inadequacy of the housing provisions of some local authorities, and "unfair methods of allocation" of houses to perpetuate Unionist control ... religious discrimination in jobs by some Unionist-controlled authorities', and gerrymandering of elections. It also found a growing and powerful sense of resentment and frustration among the Catholic population at the failure of the government to investigate and remedy complaints; resentment by Catholics of the existence of the Ulster Special Constabulary as a partisan paramilitary force recruited exclusively from Protestants; Catholic resentment about the Special Powers Act; and fears among Protestants of a threat to Unionist domination and control of government by the increase of the Catholic population.

These feelings, it seemed to me, were intensified by the actions of both Ian Paisley's Ulster Constitution Defence Committee (set up to counter republican Easter parades) and the Ulster Protestant Volunteers, a loyalist paramilitary group, which led to physical violence against civil rights demonstrators. The report also found that 'subversive elements' had cynically used the civil rights platform to stir up trouble in the streets.

Although Lord Cameron's report refrained from commenting on the role of Catholic educational facilities, he made a point of observing that 'segregated education is in many quarters regarded with regret as a real stumbling block towards better relationships between Catholics and Protestants' – something that I and others were to pursue years later in the establishment of an integrated school sector.

In October 1969 I drew the short straw of being asked to speak on behalf of the Unionist Party in the Northern Ireland debate at the Conservative Party conference at Brighton. No doubt it was felt that a Unionist MP of moderate views with a constituency comprising a fifty-fifty mix of Catholics and Protestants would provide the right image in the wake of Cameron and the increasing civil rights pressure and violence. I would have the impossible task of attempting to explain the almost unexplainable to a largely bewildered Tory conference, and to British television viewers at large. The Unionist Party was clearly on the defensive, its leadership of Northern Ireland and its right to a place within the UK being seriously questioned. Indeed, not everyone viewed Northern Ireland as part of the UK since for fifty years successive Westminster governments had tiptoed away from its affairs, allowing Stormont to do its own thing on the basis of frequent reassurances from Belfast that all was well. Outside Northern Ireland there was no real understanding of the complex nature of its politics – it was a part of the UK that did not touch everyday lives in Britain. We were a place apart.

At Brighton before that huge conference audience in the glare of high-powered lights and feeling that I was about to faint, I acknowledged that the need to send British troops in numbers to Northern Ireland would not be easily understood or found generally acceptable, but I assured the conference that the troops would be there no longer than the time it took to restore order. I confessed that the Northern Ireland situation was a very grave one. Recent months had shown how easily a spark could ignite a blaze amongst fearful and suspicious people. We had to weigh our words very carefully and above all be realistic. Northern Ireland folk, I said, were no more belligerent, no more wicked, no more unneighbourly than their fellow citizens in Britain, but they were caught in the toils of fear, and imprisoned by a heavy burden of history.

I said that I agreed with Lord Cameron that people had reacted with violence because they believed on both sides that vital issues were at stake. The issue of human rights was a big issue in any society, and so it should be. But the questions of loyalty, of allegiance, of constitutional integrity were also big issues, and Ulster Unionists would take it for granted that they would continue to be British and so would their children and their children's children. In the present situation, however, the need to create a new basis of trust was so self-evident that, as far as possible, the structures of government had to be made visibly foolproof against even a suspicion of improper bias. I was satisfied that the Stormont government was determined to do by legislation all that legislation could do. But I accepted that something more was needed than statutes of law. There had to be a revolution of feeling, and both communities had to move out of their entrenched positions and be prepared for acts of faith and trust.

I submitted that there were very positive ways in which Great Britain could help. For example, I hoped that if the Conservatives were returned to government, they would want to support measures to secure for Northern Ireland British standards in housing and employment, which would mean a willingness to allocate national resources to that end because I believed that all along economic causes had much to do with our troubles.

As regards relations with the Irish Republic, I said that I felt we had to avoid any talk of flamboyant initiatives in that field. What made the border so distinctive was the fact that the communities North and South had moved apart as the South had moved away from Britain. There was no reason why that course should not be reversed. It would not be dramatic, and must not be. We as Unionists would never agree to sever our links with Britain, but that need not preclude a decent relationship with the Irish Republic based on mutual trust and understanding.

Sitting down to modest applause I was followed by an unimpressed and less-than-generous Quintin Hogg (later Lord Hailsham). With a measure of exasperation he judged the solution to our problems to be a spiritual one. He directed the attention of Northern Ireland people to the saving grace to be found in the qualities of 'charity' as defined by St Paul. I was surprised that someone with his Ulster roots seemed to ignore the fact that the people of Northern Ireland were the victims of their own history and that the outbreak of violence had complex political causes. His answer to it all, however commendably moral, alas, was unrealistic and scarcely helpful. The reality was that there was a large (guilty but decent) moderate silent majority who hoped it would all blow over and whose fears of change and uncertainty somehow had still to be allayed. Hogg's homily was too much for Robin Chichester-Clark, the Northern Ireland Westminster MP for Derry (brother of the prime minister), who got up from his seat among the Conservative high command and left the platform.

Northern Ireland must indeed have been an enigma to the unenlightened of the outside world. A friend, Dr Robin Glasscock, a senior lecturer in Geography at Queen's University, told me of a student from California who asked to come and stay with him to see a Twelfth of July Orange parade. They waited on the Lisburn Road along which the Belfast Orange lodges would march on their way from Carlisle Circus to the Field at Finaghy – a distance of about ten miles. As usual, crowds lined the route on either side, sitting on chairs and benches, in patient expectation. Woe to any man, woman or child who tried to cross that road from one side to the other until the procession, which would take several hours, had completely gone by. To Robin's horror his guest, a huge young man in a white T-shirt with 'Santa Barbara' written across his broad back, his shoulders festooned with camera equipment, without warning strode out into the middle of the road. Facing an oncoming, particularly well-turned-out lodge of granite-faced bowler-hatted Orangemen wearing splendid collarettes, white gloves, and silver swords at the slope, the American walked backwards and, crouching as he filmed, shouted across: 'Hey, Rab. Which ones are the Catholics?'

Another difficult engagement came late in October when I was asked to speak at the annual general meeting of the South Down Unionist Association. The Hunt Report had just been published, recommending an unarmed Royal Ulster Constabulary (RUC), replacement of the controversial Ulster Special Constabulary (the B Specials) by a new part-time force under the army General Officer Commanding, and the setting up of a Police Reserve. The resentment and anger these proposals caused was palpable amongst the South Down Unionists that night in the Dundrum parish hall.

When I arrived I was greeted by Captain Willie Orr, the local Westminster MP, whose hospitality I had enjoyed on his Thames houseboat after the recent Conservative Party conference. He was an Imperial Grand Master of the Orange Order and had revived the Orange Lodge (LOL 1688) in the Westminster House of Commons in 1955. The annual general meeting was one of the rare occasions that brought him back to his constituency. He knew what I was in for because after the election of the new officers for the ensuing year (it was then about 11 p.m.), having introduced me to the assembled company, he excused himself pleading that he had a pressing engagement elsewhere. I had been warned earlier by one of the officials that there might be trouble, and to give me some protection a communion rail had been placed in front of the platform.

I had come armed with reassuring statistics on the substantial amounts of explosives, arms and ammunition uncovered recently by the RUC. I had scarcely finished my first sentence when an attractive girl sitting midway up the hall got to her feet and denounced me for what I had recently said on TV about the Reverend Ian Paisley. (I think I had suggested that he had lied about something, and I had already received – amongst the many – a hate letter warning me: 'Touch not the Lord's anointed.') I shall always be grateful to one member of the Orange Order, which was ranged on one side, who rose and told her to sit down as they wanted to hear me on Hunt's proposals. So she did, and I continued with my speech.

I played down the proposals, saying they wouldn't make a significant difference to our ability to deal effectively with the security situation –

and that we couldn't go on as we were without responding to many of the demands for reform. We had to put our house in order. The main message was that the Union was and always would be secure but that we had responsibilities for all the people of Northern Ireland of whatever class or creed. I was listened to attentively and civilly but all in all it was not a good evening. On my way to Dundrum I had been driven into by a motorist from behind when passing through Ballynahinch – 'When sorrows come, they come, not single spies, / But in battalions.'

At this time Harry West, a large-scale farmer in County Fermanagh and one-time minister of agriculture, had become the moving spirit behind a large pressure group, the West Ulster Unionist Council. It opposed reforms as weakening unionism and the position of the Northern Ireland government. In particular it opposed changes to local government and the setting up of a central housing authority. The bulk of the council's membership was made up of Unionist associations in west Ulster, but it had the support of several constituency associations in Belfast and east Ulster. It was a formidable and troublesome organisation frequently attacked by us liberal Unionists as a divisive force. Harry West insisted that it spoke for the majority of grassroots Unionists. We, on the other hand, maintained that the vast majority of the people of Northern Ireland had given the government a mandate to carry out the reforms and that the government was being responsible and forward-looking. The attempt to alienate the people from supporting those policies was in our view deplorable, and we insisted that members of parliament should instead concentrate their energies on providing homes and jobs and on educational and industrial development. In a speech to my Unionist association I claimed (amongst other things) that at a time when a reasonable and common-sense approach to our problems was vital, we were being plagued by political dinosaurs who rampaged the country in a campaign of denigration which could only bring about a major crisis in our affairs. I asked whether it could be that more houses and a fair allocation system that might mean decent living standards for all and not just some was what they opposed, and if so was this not to be taken as a declaration of principle on their part? Moreover, I asked:

Is it possible that these people are determined that democracy will not survive here if democracy means a fair deal for all? That never, if they can manage it, will they surrender one inch of what they consider to be the prerogatives of the master race?

And that never, even should they destroy this country, would they admit that very many of us have grown out of this thinking of fifty years ago?

The speech was generally well received in my own association and got a good coverage in the press. The only adverse reaction was a good-humoured one from Harry West who did not take kindly to being referred to as a dinosaur.

These views were on one side of a developing split which threatened to rock the Unionist Party, and which forced Unionist candidates at the Westminster election in June 1970 to declare openly whether they fully supported the policies of the Chichester-Clark government. There was little doubt at the time that the reluctance of Unionist candidates to give unequivocal backing to the government, particularly on the law-and-order issue, was based on fear of losing the support of 'Paisleyite-type' voters.

On 29 May 1970, Anne Dickson, Robin Bailie and I wrote a letter to the South Antrim Imperial Unionist Association:

We are very mindful of the various challengers to our party in the forthcoming general election contest in South Antrim – recently underlined by its loss of two Stormont seats in the Imperial division to the Unionist cause, in the recent by-elections. We believe it is imperative to choose a candidate who will win the respect and support of the general body of Unionist voters in the constituency, and for whom our help will be most effective in winning the votes of those who gave each of us their endorsement with large majorities in the Stormont election last year.

It is vital, too, we believe, in the interests of Ulster, that the Unionist member for South Antrim at Westminster will be one on whom Major Chichester-Clark, both as leader of the Party and Prime Minister, can rely for general support.

In fact no such assurance was asked for by the prime minister, and in the event James Molyneaux was chosen as Unionist candidate for South Antrim. The inscrutable, unflappable James Molyneaux (now Lord Molyneaux), the self-styled 'dull dog' of politics, was hardly ever likely to be in the forefront of necessary social reform. As Deputy Grand Master of the Orange Order and Sovereign Commonwealth Grand Master of the Royal Black Institution he could do no other than stand on the status quo of things. (Molyneaux was to become party leader in 1979, and he held this position for the greater part of the Troubles. From his political background and perspectives he was hardly likely to become a visionary, and whilst some of us were convinced that he was simply staving off the inevitable decline in the general attractiveness and influence of the Ulster Unionist Party, it is only fair to observe that he did moderate the effect of Paisleyism on the party and prevented Paisley from seizing control of it. Paisley never ever got the better of him.)

At the June 1970 Westminster general election, a storm blew up when Ian Paisley alleged that after talks 'at the highest level', he had reached a pact with the Unionist Party that he would not put up Protestant-Unionist candidates in South Down, Armagh and Londonderry. The Unionist side of the deal was not to attack the Paisleyites – an agreement that would have been kept had Anne Dickson, Robin Bailie and I not gone to see the prime minister at Stormont on 11 June and obtained from him an assurance that deals had not been done with the Paisleyites. It was claimed at the time that we had offered our resignations to the prime minister, which was untrue.

We continued the battle for the hearts and minds of the Unionist Party whenever we could. We hit out at the ultra-Unionists who clung to the idea that nothing had changed, that unionism was exclusively for Protestants, and that Britain would be prepared to back them through thick and thin. We believed they were wrong, dangerously wrong. There could be no going back from the conciliatory policies already in train, or Britain would be forced to intervene directly with uncertain consequences for the link itself.

Addressing the Cromac Young Unionists in Belfast on 13 November 1970, I said that the people of Britain were getting impatient with us and that there was growing questioning of our right to stay in the UK.

I hoped our UK fellow citizens believed we were worth bothering about, and accordingly we had an obligation to show ourselves worthy of British citizenship. But this would not be achieved by aggressive assertion that Unionists were entitled to stay British under any circumstances. Many of my audience could not have conceived of a situation arising that would lead us to be booted out of the UK. But they listened patiently and indulgently.

Meanwhile, in April the Alliance Party had been launched. Its members were people unknown in politics and it had no past reputation to hinder it. The party quickly gained support from a section of Unionists who had backed Terence O'Neill and who felt that Alliance now represented their outlook. Although its members were originally mostly middle-class, it attracted many people who had formerly backed the Northern Ireland Labour Party. I publicly regretted the loss to the Unionist Party of those who had been wooed away, but privately accepted that if the party at its constituency levels did not wish to have candidates of moderate views, then moderate people would start looking elsewhere.

One evening, three of the Alliance Party's founding members, Oliver Napier, Robert Cooper and Basil Glass, called at my home to discuss the possibility of me resigning from the Unionist Party and joining Alliance. For the vast majority of Unionists the Unionist Party was the traditional medium for the expression of their philosophy. Three important considerations made me reluctant to take this step. First, I was convinced that the future of the people of Northern Ireland depended upon attracting Catholics to the Unionist Party as we carried through the reforms necessary to create a just society. There were already some Catholic party members. One was Dr John White, a distinguished political scientist at Queen's University who was a regular attender at my Unionist Association meetings at Finaghy and a staunch supporter of mine. Second, I believed that I would be of more use fighting within the Unionist Party where there were people to be convinced. Finally, I felt that to walk away would be to walk out into the wilderness, as I did not believe that a nonsectarian party in Northern Ireland would get anywhere. Moreover, I had the full support of my constituency association and felt that it would be treacherous to leave.

Many people had worked hard addressing, licking and stamping envelopes and tramping the streets to get me elected. I was under no pressure or criticism at the time to tone down my radical views. I declined the invitation, which my three visitors understood but regretted, expressing the hope that I might join the new party in the future.

Two years later the Alliance Party was given a considerable boost when three sitting MPs did join its ranks: Phelim O'Neill, a former minister of agriculture, Bertie McConnell, the pro-O'Neill but Independent member for Bangor, and Tom Gormley, an Independent Nationalist.

The year 1970 was not encouraging for the liberal Unionist reform programme, which included the disbanding of the B Specials as recommended by the Hunt report and the reform of local government along the lines of the Macrory report. It was hoped these measures would resolve the Northern Ireland problem, but perversely they were accompanied by a steady deterioration of relations between Protestants and Catholics. Throughout the summer the Provisional IRA carried out a bombing campaign aimed at setting the agenda for Catholic politics. They calculated (rightly as it turned out) that increased violence would lead to the collapse of Stormont, which they saw as the first step to a united Ireland. The unremitting violence of the early 1970s, despite the reforms, suggested that those reforms were historically too late. The initiative was not with the government but with the IRA, which exploited flaws in Unionist single-party rule. Each day brought its own crisis. There was little a liberal Unionist could say that was helpful in such a volatile situation, with deaths from shootings and bombings continuing unabated. Any light at the end of the tunnel had already been blown out.

These were miserable gloomy days for me. The only consolation I had was the wholehearted support of a patient, long-suffering Jill, who courageously and enthusiastically played her part as an MP's wife, attending often difficult constituency and public meetings with a good grace. On the occasions when it was necessary, and they were many, she entertained at 2 Cherryvalley Park, putting on splendid dinners as only she could do, skilfully disguising that we were really rather poor. I was desperately trying to keep in touch with my profession, but could never guarantee the solicitor that I would be available when I was needed.

We were very fortunate by now to have three amenable, uncomplicated and cooperative children. Jonathan and Timothy were day boys at Campbell College a short distance away, and Jane was at Ashleigh, across on the south side of Belfast. There was one exciting fringe benefit available to a Unionist backbencher which helped us to forget, albeit briefly, the intolerable tension. This was the invitation to attend Commonwealth parliamentary conferences around the world, all expenses paid. It was a matter of Buggin's turn, and colleagues who had been to Gibraltar or Kuala Lumpur or Canberra or Auckland or Fiji on one of these junkets assured me that my turn would come. It seemed that the allocation was in the hands of Lord Glentoran, the Speaker of the Senate. Visions I might have had of tropical skies and waving palm trees were shattered when I was invited by him to lead a parliamentary deputation to the House of Keyes on the Isle of Man.

It was an atrocity in March 1971 that led to the resignation of Chichester-Clark as prime minister. Three off-duty Scottish soldiers of the Royal Highland Fusiliers, two of them brothers aged seventeen and eighteen, were lured from a pub by members of the Provisional IRA and murdered on the outskirts of Belfast. This was the signal for a new loyalist campaign demanding Chichester-Clark's resignation.

Chichester-Clark flew to London on 18 March but failed to persuade Ted Heath, the prime minister, to deal more firmly with the rapidly deteriorating security situation. Rioting, the creation of no-go areas, increased killing of soldiers, RUC personnel and members of the UDR (the Ulster Defence Regiment which had replaced the B Specials) had made Chichester-Clark's position precarious. Two days later he resigned, and was replaced by the firmer Brian Faulkner.

5

THE NEW MAN

IT WAS ROUND THE FIGURE OF Brian Faulkner that the hopes of Protestant liberals now centred. Although he had long been regarded by us as something of a hardliner, I am satisfied that in the end he was a genuine convert to substantial reform in the mould established by O'Neill. A most able and skilful politician, Faulkner epitomised those Ulster Unionists who were wise or at least pragmatic enough to see the need for liberal reforms. With hindsight only such a person, coming from within the ranks of mainstream unionism and with irreproachable Orange credentials, rather than one of the few 'genuine' liberals, could have carried significant Protestant support on the road to powersharing.

Faulkner's defeat of William Craig, the recognised leader of right-wing Unionism, for the Unionist Party leadership and therefore the premiership was convincing. I have reason to remember that day, 19 March 1971. I had received a telephone call from home that my mother had been taken ill. I was in the Bar Library at the time. I had arranged that evening to take my mother to a function in the Knock Methodist church and can remember her that morning rushing out for a hairdo at Cherryvalley village in perfectly good health so far as I could see. I sensed from the tone of the caller, our daily help Mrs Ena Long, that my mother was more than just ill. I found her dead on the kitchen floor. I made what arrangements I could and left for Stormont. It was a sign of the madness of those times that for ten minutes a party election had to take precedence.

At Stormont I cast my vote in the leadership election, in which Brian Faulkner defeated William Craig by twenty-six votes to four. Faulkner announced his cabinet on 25 March. It included Harry West as minister of agriculture. Faulkner's thinking was that raising hopes of unionist solidarity might isolate Craig and Paisley. Faulkner balanced the return of West with the appointment of David Bleakley, a member of the Northern Ireland Labour Party, as minister of community relations.

To us liberals, always wary of Faulkner, the appointment of West appeared to be a distinct lurch to the right, and Anne Dickson resigned from the parliamentary party in protest. For my part, I did not like the selection but understood the reasons behind it and I was satisfied that Faulkner was determined to continue with the reform policies. What I now believe he was essentially trying to do was adopt a strong line in security as a basis for political reform. He was above all being realistic about the possibilities of persuading Protestants of the need for political change when bombs were exploding regularly on the streets of Belfast and Derry.

At a meeting of Finaghy and Malone Unionists, and later on television, I questioned the advisability of Faulkner's choice of a cabinet which I believed did not present the widest possible appeal to the community at large. I said it was an act of political misjudgement by a man I thought would have been a good deal more intelligent. Later I was reminded by him that he reserved the right to decide who should serve with him in the government, and that it was a right he must be free to exercise.

August 1971 saw Northern Ireland on the brink of civil war. Ethnic cleansing had begun. The introduction of internment without trial by Brian Faulkner on 9 August was followed by a dramatic increase in violence. Protestants were forced out of the Ardoyne area of Belfast, setting fire to two hundred houses as they left rather than leave them unoccupied for Catholics to take over. By 12 August up to 7,000 people (the majority Catholics) had been left homeless as houses were burned to the ground. Some 2,500 Catholics left Belfast for refugee camps set up in the Republic; 2,000 Protestants were left homeless. Barricades were set up in Catholic working-class areas and both the Provisionals and the Official IRA engaged in gun battles with the army in Belfast. In the words of one commentator, the introduction of internment triggered off 'waves of deaths, street disruptions and political and social fragmentation on a major scale'.

My constituency received a lot of attention in the dawn sweeps by the army. I found my profile raised when it was discovered (or remembered) that I was chairman of the Northern Ireland Group of Amnesty International. Radio Free Belfast, broadcasting from the Falls Road every hour on the hour, advised relatives of internees to contact me for help to rescue their loved ones. Jill was receiving frequent telephone calls from some of my Andersonstown constituents who complained, 'There's Basil McIvor getting niggers out of gaol, and our wee Hughie, walkin' down the Crumlin Road, was lifted for nothin!'

In September, David Bleakley resigned from the cabinet a few days before his six months' term of office had expired; his resignation was in protest at the introduction of internment and the failure to introduce new political initiatives. Four weeks later, on 26 October, I received a telephone call from Robert Ramsay, the prime minister's private secretary, to say that the prime minister wanted to see me. I had a fair idea why. Discussing with Jill the possibility that Faulkner might ask me to replace Bleakley, we both agreed that I should decline because of Harry West's presence in the cabinet.

The prime minister was at his chirpiest, businesslike best when I was ushered into his room at Stormont Castle and walked towards a deep, comfortable armchair into which I sank, thus putting myself at an immediate disadvantage. From that position I needed all the determination I could muster to dismiss the blandishments.

With him it seemed all very much in the day's business. Outside, the community was rapidly moving in the direction of civil war, yet he was cheerfully reassuring with his 'no problems' attitude. Would I join his cabinet? I had been turning over in my mind what my response should be and the reasons for it; I had been reminding myself where I stood in the political spectrum *vis-à-vis* the hardliners. I had given no hawkish sop to comfort right-wing hearts. But then, my constituency was different. A moderate middle-class Catholic community had allowed me the freedom of stretching my liberal political life. We discussed my reluctance to join an administration that had in it someone who was diametrically opposed to my political stance. I said that I therefore had to decline the invitation. Furthermore, I preferred to have the freedom to pursue my line, unfettered, outside government – and, anyway, I was not 'cabinet material'.

The PM would have none of it. He accepted the validity of my views on the way forward, and said he knew that I supported the constitution, had not offended others (Catholics in particular), was not a member of any politico-religious organisation, and had a long-standing interest in community relations. My credentials for the post of minister of community relations thus appeared to him to be just right.

I asked myself what sort of fool I was to imagine for one second that I could afford to refuse when I was being offered the best medium through which I could promote my views – where it was all at, in government! Within five minutes of my arrival I had accepted. My appointment was announced that day. Next day I was duly sworn in to the Northern Ireland Privy Council by the Governor of Northern Ireland, Lord Grey. In the Stormont parliament all cabinet ministers were appointed to the Privy Council for life.

Once inside the Stormont cabinet I found that the reality of government was close to the cynical reply of television's fictional Sir Humphrey Appleby to his new minister of administrative affairs, the Right Honourable Jim Hacker MP: when Jim enthusiastically declared his belief that the ultimate purpose of government was doing good, Sir Humphrey's reply was, 'Minister, government isn't about good and evil, it's only about order and chaos. It isn't about morality, it's about stability, keeping things going, preventing anarchy, stopping society falling to bits, still being there tomorrow.'

The ministry of community relations had been established on 29 October 1969 on the initiative of James Callaghan, then home secretary responsible for Northern Ireland affairs, in line with a commitment given in a joint communiqué of the British and Northern Ireland governments on 29 August to designate a minister to have special responsibility for community relations. The department's function was to monitor action to put the communiqué into practice, to advise other departments on the community relations aspect of their work, and to assist the newly established Community Relations Commission and administer payments to projects designed to improve social amenities in urban areas suffering from social deprivation. Given the tensions arising out of house searches by the army, when floorboards were lifted in the constant search for arms, explosives and radio equipment, we appointed five civil representatives to go into each house after a raid to arrange for repair of damage as quickly as possible, in conjunction with the army.

Maurice Hayes was the first chairman of the Community Relations Commission. I got the distinct impression that he was not at all anxious for the department to be seen to be involved at the sharp end or doubling up on the work the commission was doing. In his view, the commission was the appropriate agency for close-quarter activity.

Sir Harold Black, secretary to the cabinet, and his deputy at the time, Ken Bloomfield, had to appear to be very supportive of the new ministry but well understood the size and complexity of the task. Because it was new, the department had no officials with relevant experience and there was no historical basis on which to strike a budget. Nevertheless, Callaghan regarded it as important and therefore a matter of policy that there should be a minister responsible to the Stormont parliament for money spent on community relations initiatives. Ian Paisley, then chairman of the Public Accounts Committee, would certainly want to be satisfied with the even-handedness of the deployment of taxpayers' money.

Importantly, in 1970, before my arrival, the ministry of community relations had been responsible for the passing of the Social Need (Grants) Act enabling the ministry to pay grants to local authorities, statutory authorities or other persons to cover expenditure incurred by them because of the existence in any urban area of special social need. This Act was a godsend – it gave the ministry something positive to do.

To the public I immediately made it clear that I had no illusions about the situation in Northern Ireland. There was no magic formula for better community relations. To think that I or anyone else could suddenly reverse a situation that had prevailed for generations would be folly. I could not make one man love his neighbour, still less sort out a whole community's problem. My line was that community relations was an intangible thing. It was not something that could be provided, like schools or roads or hospitals. Nor could it be imposed. I thought of my new role as largely presentational. The most I could hope to do was to make people realise they had a problem, that it was a soluble problem but that only they could solve it.

That there was a problem was all too evident. Not a single night at the time did not bring its share of explosions and riots, and almost every day dawned on the aftermath of destruction and death. There was no political answer to the gunman. The terrorists causing anarchy had only one end – the destruction of the state. They would not be prepared to accept a democratic solution, nor would they be moved by argument or rational appeal. It was clear that deliberate attempts were being made to provoke Protestants to violence; communal violence would make the work of terrorists much easier. The spirit of restraint and lack of response to provocation displayed by the Protestant population up to then was impressive. Whilst there was no room for doubt about the rights and wrongs of terrorism, political and social conflicts were much more complicated. A sense of realism was needed to decide what the real priorities and objectives were, which I believed to be a joint effort in which all citizens of Northern Ireland were equal partners. My role was to try to ensure that people were aware of the alternatives.

Out and about around Northern Ireland I attended the funerals of murdered policemen and UDR men and visited their relatives. Coming away late in the evening from Portora Royal School in Enniskillen, I heard over the car radio of the attempted assassination by the IRA of my cabinet colleague John Taylor, minister of state for home affairs; this brought home to me for the first time the dangers of public office. On the way home I went to the border area to visit a grieving young wife whose husband, a member of the UDR, had been shot dead the previous day. For the next twenty-five years, on and off for lengthy periods, I was seldom free from the presence of a bodyguard.

On 4 December 1971, accompanied by my son Jonathan, I visited the hospital where Pat McGurk and his son lay seriously injured. Pat McGurk's North Queen Street bar in Belfast had been bombed by the Ulster Volunteer Force (UVF): fifteen men, women and children, including his wife and daughter, died as a result of the blast, and thirteen were injured – the greatest loss of civilian life in Northern Ireland resulting from a single incident. A huge charge of gelignite had exploded inside the pub on the ground floor, bringing hundreds of tons of rubble crashing down on customers – the explosion was heard as far away as Carrickfergus. Reports had come in of soldiers, police officers, firemen and hundreds of civilians clawing in the rubble with their hands to search for survivors, of small fires breaking out as the rescue operation got under way, and of screams echoing through the darkness as badly mutilated bodies were pulled out of the wreckage. In the hospital we saw many of the victims, red eyes staring out of bandages, fearfully burnt, Pat McGurk's son encased in bandages lying near his father. Pat knew that his wife and daughter were amongst the dead, yet he said to me, 'If this brings peace to Northern Ireland, I am prepared to accept it.' Pat's hopes have yet to be realised. This incident recruited many youngsters to the Provisional IRA.

In the intensive care ward of the Royal Victoria Hospital in March 1972, I visited victims of the bombing of the Abercorn restaurant in the centre of Belfast, in which 2 people were killed and 130 were injured, including two sisters who had been shopping for a wedding dress, each of whom lost both legs. At the bedside of one of the girls was her boyfriend; they subsequently married. Nearby was a badly wounded IRA terrorist and a dying soldier.

At around that time, I had an opportunity to confront Ruairí Ó Brádaigh, the Sinn Féin president, about the horror and carnage for which the IRA was responsible. I happened to be appearing on a television programme in Boston, Massachusetts, called *The Advocates*. The question for debate on that occasion was 'Should the United States support the unification of Ireland?' The other participants were John Hume of the SDLP, Michael O'Kennedy (parliamentary secretary for education in the Republic), Brian Faulkner (on film), Bill Craig (leader of the newly formed Ulster Vanguard), Dr Noel Browne (former minister of health in the Republic), Oliver Napier (leader of the Alliance Party) and the American politician Michael Dukakis.

I took Ó Brádaigh aside afterwards and asked him what civilised philosophy could possibly justify what I had seen. He replied with no obvious cynicism, 'What must be, must be'. He then went off to collect from his briefcase a pamphlet entitled *Éire Nua* which he handed to me – this outlined Sinn Féin's policy at that time of a federal Ireland (later to be scrapped by Gerry Adams and the new Sinn Féin blood in favour of a constitutional policy). I did not expect to find Ruairí Ó Brádaigh the courteous, warm character he turned out to be – he had some personal charm. He explained to me that the new Ireland would be a four-province federal Ireland with maximum devolution, power being decentralised to regional and local communities. As the Unionists would have a clear majority in the North, they would not be ruled from Dublin but would, in all regional matters, govern themselves. Everyone born on the island of Ireland, he said, should have access to power and decision making. As to getting to this situation, he was adamantly opposed to Sinn Féin becoming involved in democratic politics. *Éire Nua* stood the best chance, he said, of getting 'the Brits out' – which was the paramount consideration.

Early in 1972, accompanied by Jill, I attended the National Prayer Breakfast in the Hilton Hotel, Washington, organised by the world-wide Christian Leadership Fellowship which I had joined in 1969. This movement had been formed to develop and maintain an informal association of responsible lay men and women banded together to find through Christianity a better way of living in order to promote for home, community, nation, the world, and at every level of society a leadership led by God – to be and to build bridges of communication and understanding between people. From this movement, when

General Eisenhower was president, there had emerged the National Prayer Breakfast. In February each year since then, at a time near the opening of Congress, members of the US Senate and House of Representatives involved in the fellowship movement have invited politicians and policy makers from every state and every nation to join the president of the United States 'in this time together'. To this day at the time of the breakfast, hundreds of people and groups throughout the world meet to pray for their nations and their leaders. Westminster now has its own prayer breakfast. I arranged one at Stormont when Brian Faulkner was prime minister.

The Golden Ballroom of the Hilton Hotel presented a dazzling spectacle at the 1972 breakfast. Almost the entire US administration was there on the platform behind President Nixon. Over in the corner a university choir was singing 'Amazing Grace'. It was a typical US production designed to melt the hardest heart and bring together the most intransigent enemies in a warm glow of brotherly love and concern.

My engagements included an hour-long private discussion with John Niedaker, one of Nixon's special personal assistants, an informal meeting with Dr Billy Graham, who had visited us at home in Belfast, and a luncheon speech to the Washington Breakfast Group, an influential body of leading judges, lawyers, businessmen and academics. This was a splendid opportunity to explain the true nature of what was happening in Northern Ireland and to put it into the context of violence as part of an international phenomenon that the United States would understand.

It was just as well the note from the British embassy that was passed to me by those guests on my right did not reach me before I had made my speech, which was to be dramatically overtaken by the events in Derry on Sunday, 30 January. The note read starkly: '13 men shot dead and 17 wounded by the Parachute Regiment in Derry.'

In the afternoon the British ambassador, Lord Cromer, asked to see me. He felt that as minister of community relations I might feel it wise to return home immediately, more especially because the embassy had had a request from Edward Kennedy who, on hearing of this incident, was calling for the immediate withdrawal of British troops from Northern Ireland. He had asked the embassy to arrange for me to discuss the matter with him on television that evening. Of course, I knew nothing of the circumstances leading up to what had happened in Derry and in any case would clearly have been on a hiding to nothing facing such an influential senator on his own patch debating an event that he would exploit on behalf of his Irish lobby. Fred Corbett, my press officer, hastily called a news conference at which I expressed my own personal deep sorrow at the tragic incidents in Derry but said I could not comment in detail. I was asked directly about the statement issued by Senator Kennedy calling for the withdrawal of troops, and I could only say that the Stormont government was agreed on the desirability of getting troops off the streets of Belfast and Derry, and that this would start just as soon as the IRA stopped its campaign of death and destruction and when people decided to live within the democratic law of Northern Ireland.

A scheduled VC10 flight to London from Dulles Airport was delayed and the ambassadorial Rolls was pressed into service to whisk me to the airport: Lord Cromer had achieved his aim of getting me out of the way. Jill, who was then a law librarian and on the board of the International Association of Law Librarians, remained behind to fulfil an engagement with colleagues in the Library of Congress.

I arrived back to a bitterly cold day of frequent sleet showers, and immediately made my way up to Stormont. There the prime minister said cheerfully: 'I thought you were in Washington!' I was mystified that what had happened in Derry was not being viewed with much more concern – so far as I could see.

Bloody Sunday was a defining moment, the beginning of the end of Stormont. It created a wave of anger which swept through the now totally alienated Catholic community. A torrent of international criticism of Britain followed which led Ted Heath to set up an inquiry into the killings headed by the Lord Chief Justice, Lord Widgery. Maurice Hayes, as a prominent Catholic, resigned his chairmanship of the Community Relations Commission. He has observed in his book *Minority Verdict* that he 'could not be even vicariously the representative and defender of a government that shot its citizens on the streets'. It is never too late to attempt to restore faith and trust by an apology from the British government for the events of that dreadful day in Derry. It is healthy to confront the past.

The west Belfast Catholic housing estate of Ballymurphy was the centre of serious rioting in 1971 and 1972. Mother Teresa of Calcutta and her Sisters of Mercy attempted to set up a mission there in late 1971. On a visit to Belfast in February 1972, she came to ask me if I could find accommodation in the area for her Sisters to run open houses where they might look after 'latchkey' children until parents arrived home from work, and instruct young mothers in needlework, in the use of sewing machines, and in household skills. Mother Teresa's main concern was to get children off the streets.

It was a raw day with persistent rain when Mother Teresa – a tiny, gaunt, round-shouldered figure with sparkling eyes and a palpable radiance – came to our home at Cherryvalley Park. She had with her two young Sisters with incredibly clear and beautiful complexions. They emerged from a white Volkswagen Beetle, in open sandals, wearing their blue-trimmed white saris. Their only material possessions in this world were two saris each and a bucket in which to wash the sari not in use.

We had a cheerful fire going, in front of which settee and chairs were arranged invitingly around. They allowed themselves to enjoy the warmth of the fire. Jill was concerned about what to produce for afternoon tea – a balance had to be struck between welcoming a greatly honoured guest and not appearing too lavish in the presence of such a saintly person. Our modest sitting room suddenly seemed overfurnished and somehow decadent. The Sisters ate with enjoyment but Mother Teresa only drank a little tea. Even after they had left, we still felt the presence of saintliness. It seemed inappropriate for the children to be allowed to watch television until a decent interval had elapsed!

In the course of our conversation she had told us in her characteristic forthright way that she found children in Ballymurphy more spiritually deprived and less responsive than those dying in her arms in the streets of Calcutta. The little mission lasted less than a year. The manner of the Sisters' going is something about which it is only possible to speculate. But I do know that they were sadly missed by the local population.

Meanwhile, the unrelenting IRA pressure continued, with no-warning bombs and with hoax calls deliberately leading shoppers towards the area where the bombs were planted. Talk of reform was politically difficult. Attempts to patch up the Stormont administration by, for example, creating by statutory means an entrenched position in the cabinet for members of the Catholic community as such would probably, it was thought, strengthen sectarian divisions and make difficult attempts to create nonsectarian political alignments.

With the support of the Unionist Party, Faulkner had suggested the establishment of three new functional committees, in addition to the existing Public Accounts Committee, of which the opposition would always hold at least two of the salaried chairmanships. These committees would be involved in policy making at the formative stage, in reviewing and testing the performance of the executive, and in giving expert consideration to legislation. Privy councillorships were to be on offer to those heading the committees. Paddy Devlin regarded the proposals as 'Faulker's greatest hour'. But again it was too little too late.

I had expressed my view on this in the House in June 1971, saying that single-party government created enormous difficulties for MPs on both sides; that I understood well the feelings of frustration and despair that the opposition must have, knowing that as things were they could never hope to be in power, but that so long as this parliament had power to determine the constitutional status of Northern Ireland that situation would continue. I had said that I hoped that opportunities for participation in government through this revolutionary system of house committees would get a matching response.

I shared the belief of not a few: that the fundamental political problem in Northern Ireland was that of creating a participatory democracy. It was the *de facto* exclusion of almost all Catholics and some Protestants from relevant political activity that kept alive the nationalist cause and that produced the frustration that exploded in phenomena such as the civil rights movement. I thought it wrong to exclude; I also thought it extremely inexpedient. Quite apart from the social harmony that participation would bring and the political talent that might be available, there was the risk that the continued agitation of movements such as People's Democracy would eventually, for want of anything better, tack recognition of the rights of nationhood onto the bottom of its list of demands. Unless an opportunity for participation were to be created, social disorder would irrevocably polarise our society.

So how could participation be achieved? Previously Harry Calvert had written a pleading letter to Robin Bailie, Anne Dickson and myself to the effect that the best method was not via a new unionist party but by splitting the Ulster Unionist Party and annihilating the reactionary, undemocratic thinking associated with the hardliners 'which found their voice only because of the lack of interest of moderate people at local association level'. At the time, the New Ulster Movement (NUM) led by Peter Campbell was working away at building a new party. Whilst Peter Campbell was an able and pleasant person, Harry felt he was a born loser, and that in any event, the NUM had no roots. Harry consequently had no great faith in its ability to succeed. So, through a Progressive Unionist Association fronted by the three of us and like-minded others, Harry thought that before all was lost we must try to reverse at local association level the party's movement to the right. This was evidenced at the time in the Young Unionist Council elections and the Senate selections. There was no time to spare, Harry warned. Hurry, hurry! This I was afraid was all pie in the sky at a time when all our energies were absorbed in reacting to the most recent act of violence and disruption.

By spring it was too late. On 22 March 1972, Ted Heath relayed to Brian Faulkner, Jack Andrews (the deputy prime minister), Harold Black, Ken Bloomfield and Robert Ramsay at Downing Street the united view of the British cabinet, which was:

> there should be a transfer to Westminster of all security powers and responsibility for criminal matters, followed by a constitutional referendum, a move towards ending internment, the appointment of a secretary of state for Northern Ireland, and open-ended talks with the SDLP on the form of government with a view to reaching a 'community government'.

Northern Ireland had been adjudged unfit to govern itself. Next morning the Northern Ireland cabinet met in gathering gloom to discuss the impossible terms. The situation seemed unreal – was this actually happening? Harry West argued that we had no right to threaten resignation – the very thing Heath was looking for – because the electorate of Northern Ireland had placed us there to operate, on their behalf, the parliament and government that the great men of former years had so strenuously fought to establish and for which so many had given their lives. He doubted very much if Heath would risk closing down a democratically elected parliament and government.

A tense discussion took place around the long dark cabinet table as we faced up to the cold realities, the inscrutable, handsome face of Disraeli in its gilt frame on the wall looking down on our misery. Most of us were not prepared to be part of a democratic government that had not the power to legislate on matters of law and order. Central to any state is its coercive power through police or army. In the absence of such a power it cannot call itself a state. Truthfully, though, Northern Ireland, with its government devolved from Westminster, could not call itself a state; but legal niceties like this were irrelevant to those who perceived the Stormont government as having all the attributes of a state. By a majority vote, Faulkner was allowed to threaten Heath with our resignation, which was gladly accepted the following day, 24 March.

Tom Wilson, who had acted as an adviser to the Stormont government on various occasions, says in *Ulster: Conflict and Consent*:

> In retrospect, it seems probable that, from their own point of view, the Unionists were wrong in not accepting the surrender of responsibility for law and order. If the Westminster Government really wanted to hold that hot potato, they could have been allowed to do so. The Northern Ireland Parliament would then have remained in being and the Unionist position would have been a good deal stronger than it was to prove under Direct Rule.

In his letter of resignation, Brian Faulkner said that the transfer of security powers to London 'is not justifiable and cannot be supported or accepted by us. It would wholly undermine the powers, authority and standing of this government.' The introduction of direct rule from Westminster followed the suspension of Stormont, depriving the Unionist Party of control of the apparatus of government in Northern Ireland.

Just before lunch on Tuesday, 27 March, we had our last cabinet meeting. Afterwards we all trooped out through the doors that led off

the Members' Dining Room on to the balcony. We looked down on
the huge tide of people sweeping up along the mile-long drive from the
Upper Newtownards Road to Parliament Buildings. For the ordinary
Protestant the end of Stormont was the final humiliation. They
marched in their thousands that day in peaceful bewilderment at what
had happened. I heard the head of the Northern Ireland Civil Service,
Sir David Holden, standing beside me say under his breath, 'Perfidious
Albion'.

John Brooke (Viscount Brookeborough) and I left Stormont that
day through a ground-floor window on the east side of the building to
avoid the crowds, which I dodged all the way home down to Cherryvalley Park and the family, leaving behind seals of office, authority,
official car, and suffering a badly battered self-respect.

I remembered hearing that when Bob Hope was asked why he never
ran for a seat in the Senate, which there was little doubt he would have
secured, he replied, 'No sir, one day you are drinking the wine, the next
day you are picking the grapes!' I now knew what he meant.

6

THE LAST CHANCE?

ANGRY AND FRUSTRATED PROTESTANTS could not easily accept direct rule. At the end of March 1972, Brian Faulkner scornfully derided the new Westminster arrangements and rejected moves to get him to work with the new administration controlled now by the Northern Ireland Office. 'It may be an interesting – but it certainly will not be a pretty – sight when we are faced with the sort of people who will creep out to collaborate in this totally undemocratic sham,' he said.

There arose again the spectre of the Protestant backlash, as Bill Craig and his Ulster Vanguard movement held rallies across Northern Ireland – Bill arriving with motorcycle escorts clad in black leather jackets, or swooping down in a light private plane. The largest rally, in Belfast's

Ormeau Park, attracted around sixty thousand opponents of direct rule. Craig remarked at this neofascist-looking event, 'If politics fail, it will be our duty to liquidate the enemy.'

As the months passed, the British government and Willie Whitelaw, now secretary of state for Northern Ireland (dubbed by the Protestants 'Willie Whitewash'), learned that the initial softly, softly approach ('killing the IRA by kindness'), whilst boosting the moderate SDLP, could not be sustained.

One of Whitelaw's first actions was to free from detention one hundred suspected terrorists. Releases continued in succeeding weeks, reaching five hundred by early June. Areas of the Bogside and Creggan in Derry and parts of west Belfast were allowed to exist as no-go areas. To open them up would invite a bloodbath. The IRA's response was to get tougher: they tarred and feathered a pregnant woman and tied her to a lamppost for some unspecified crime. A deaf and dumb man had the same treatment some days later. They bombed heavily across Northern Ireland.

Protestant assassination gangs began to take reprisals. In the four months following direct rule, 600 bombs exploded, 2,057 people were injured, and 192 died. It emerged that Whitelaw had been talking secretly to IRA leaders and arranging for a general ceasefire, which ultimately came into effect on 26 June. Between the announcement of the ceasefire and its implementation, four days later, 10 more people died. The truce lasted until 9 July, when the IRA staged a gun battle with the army in Catholic Lenadoon, part of my former constituency.

To walk away in a huff from the new administration would in my view have been irresponsible and have exacerbated a desperate situation. I therefore decided to risk being branded a collaborator and, with some qualifications, promised my support for the Whitelaw direct rule arrangements. In doing so, I broke publicly and plainly with the official Unionist Party line and that of my erstwhile cabinet colleagues, who did not go beyond a surly acceptance of Whitelaw's rule. My argument was bread-and-butter. If, in due course, people whose only exercise was walking to the labour exchange found themselves travelling to a job, then my support would go to those who could provide this employment.

I used a meeting of the Dunmurry Unionist Association on 3 May to say that I would not join in decrying the new administration, because nothing dramatic had as yet been produced by it. I knew I would be heavily criticised for this. In my defence I said I was not casting away any principles or beliefs, but was quite simply convinced that if Northern Ireland was to have a peaceful and settled future it must work for it and in doing so cast aside some of the old historical prejudices. I commented that the violence that had taken place in Protestant east Belfast over the previous week (where several Catholics had been killed in sectarian attacks by loyalist paramilitaries) would cause British people to question seriously Northern Ireland's link with Britain.

I said I understood the frustration that led people to say, 'Apparently violence succeeds.' But what had in fact saved Northern Ireland from being utterly destroyed was the responsibility and singular restraint shown by the Protestant population during a most difficult and provocative period. I felt it would be a great tragedy if we were to descend to the level of those who used the gun to try to influence yet again the course of history in Ireland. My belief was that if we were to work through the medium of the Whitelaw administration to achieve a greater harmony between the divided sections of our community, we had to make the effort to extend the hand of friendship across the sectarian barrier. I also believed that there would be others who would respond from the other side. We could expect rebuffs, old prejudices would be rekindled, and the way forward would not be easy.

My striking out for the high moral ground when all around was anger, doom and despair irritated many of my friends, and not only those who always regarded me as a weak politician. I was awarded no points at all for these limp views which people did not want to hear at that turbulent time. An irate Roy Bradford, a former minister of commerce in the Stormont government, who was by then beginning to show signs of his ambitions to take over the leadership of the Unionist Party, phoned me wanting to know what I was up to. Had I been in touch with others about this line? Much closer to home, I received a letter from Jonathan, at that time a boarder at Campbell College. In common with virtually the entire Protestant population, he was outraged at the demise of Stormont. He had been at Bill Craig's rally against direct rule at Ormeau Park when talk of civil war was rife and the mood was volatile and menacing. Jonathan had got used to my radical tendencies, but this time he felt I had gone too far. He had read my speech in the *Irish Times*. His letter was brief and to the point:

Stalag Luft II

Dear Dad

I knew it was only a matter of time!

Jonathan

I could understand his embarrassment and disappointment with his father. The times were out of joint for my brand of politics.

On 21 July the IRA blitzed Belfast with twenty-two bombs. It was a warm summer's day and I could hear the explosions as I was cutting the hedges at home, four miles away. The worst incident was the bomb blast at Oxford Street bus station which killed eleven people and injured one hundred and thirty. That evening's television showed young policemen shovelling human remains into plastic bags. The Catholic SDLP condemned the IRA in forthright terms. The IRA made a brief, chilling statement: 'We accept responsibility.'

At the time much public criticism was levelled at the news media. It was accepted that the politicians had failed and that violence had succeeded, but also that the media had contributed to both. The ability to achieve change by political means had been swept aside and violence had proved to be the stronger weapon.

The coverage of the no-go syndrome was an example of violence breeding violence and giving it wider currency. No-go areas were those whose residents decided to create and maintain an enclave into which the forces of law and order might not go. Often this happened in areas that had been the loudest in demanding the maintenance of law and order. The media coverage of these areas was dramatic and pro-vided banner headlines; undoubtedly it led to the practice being widely emulated, adding considerably to the burden of the security forces.

Then there were examples of the press and television willingly and gullibly lending themselves to coverage of stunts, such as IRA roadblocks, or the showing of the barrel of what purported to be a Browning machine gun in an emplacement. News was, in fact, what the media chose to tell us was news. Journalists were arrogating to themselves a tremendous power and influence without, it seemed, concern for the public interest. Power without responsibility placed a very heavy onus upon those exercising it. I remember one occasion when a small brave banner was raised in a number of beleaguered areas in Belfast: people were asked to sign forms that pledged their desire for peace. In my view this initiative deserved significant media attention, but the coverage it in fact received was minuscule compared to that given to shots fired in Derry that day. Efforts for peace were more likely than not to be pushed to the bottom of the news, while efforts for war were given full news treatment.

Uniquely, the editorial policy of the *Belfast Telegraph* under its editor, Jack Sayers, was consistently and courageously to give editorial coverage to the cause of moderation and tolerance; that newspaper thereby provided much encouragement to liberal Unionists. But it was no match for the dramatic portrayal and reporting of violence elsewhere. The weapons and tactics of street warfare were covered by racing cameramen and journalists whose commitment, mainly to rapid reputation-building, shone consistently through in their writing. I can remember noting the disappointment of foreign cameramen covering one Twelfth of July when no disorder could be found throughout the day.

By chance or design, the proponents and the perpetrators of violence had found in the media their most powerful ally; while politicians helped to create the conditions for violence, the media, in many instances, helped to sustain it.

In December I found myself standing at yet another crossroads as far as my continued membership of the Unionist Party was concerned. The party had over the previous few years comprised an uneasy alliance of right wing and centre. The relationship between the Unionist Party and Bill Craig's Ulster Vanguard pressure group within the party was beginning to be seriously questioned by some of us. Bill Craig had recently said that if 'a stronger-than-heretofore Northern Ireland parliament within the United Kingdom system did not arise, or alternatively an independent constitution with a new relationship to Britain and the Commonwealth, any substitute would be opposed and destroyed by force if necessary'.

Sir Robert Porter, the former minister of home affairs, had left the Unionist Party shortly after direct rule fearing that, through its association with Vanguard, it was becoming simply a right-wing Protestant party. Others had followed him, including one of us liberals, Robin Bailie. It was essential for those of us left on the liberal wing to bring the whole question of Vanguard to a head as we believed that membership of Vanguard was incompatible with membership of the Unionist Party. In reality we were two parties within the one skin, believing different things and having different objectives. I maintained that the Unionist Party had to decide, and decide quickly, which element was to occupy the skin of unionism.

Recognising that we were entering a critical phase for the future of Northern Ireland, Brian Faulkner ultimately agreed to political talks with Willie Whitelaw. It was vital that he had the party's support for whatever his line would be. But the party was split, and it was obvious that we should face the fact that a formal parting was inevitable. If those who favoured the concept of a unilateral declaration of independence (UDI) failed themselves to leave, the party should assist them on their way. The party would inevitably lose members, but it could do without that kind of support.

Many inside the party felt that there was room for many kinds of unionism within it. But these elements threatened unionism itself. They ran the risk of alienating not only the Labour leader, Harold Wilson, who had been reflecting a growing distaste in Britain for 'the whole weary problem in Northern Ireland', but also others more favourably disposed to us who were troubled about how far they could continue with their support.

In Britain there was then an almost total misunderstanding of the unionist position. It was largely taken to be that of Bill Craig, Vanguard and the Ulster Defence Association (UDA). Within the Unionist Party John Taylor, who had recovered from the assassination attempt, had been strongly espousing the cause of independence, brushing aside the economic implications. Captain William Long, a former minister of education, on the other hand, was urging that there must be a total denunciation of UDI, not only for economic reasons, but also because unionists believed that their future was inextricably linked to the rest of the UK. These were the views of two political parties, not one.

A motion calling for disaffiliation of Vanguard supporters from the Unionist Party came before the party's policy-making Standing Committee on 11 December at a meeting in the Park Avenue Hotel, Belfast. It was moved by Stratton Mills, Westminster MP for North Belfast, and seconded by myself. We had briefly discussed our tactics beforehand. It was an unpleasant meeting, with heckling and foot stamping (a conventional and menacing method of disapproval) and some of the three hundred delegates demanded that Stratton should leave the party.

Supporters of the motion included Roy Bradford. Among the many who spoke against were Bill Craig, Martin Smyth (then County Grand Master of the Orange Lodge of Belfast), Captain Austin Ardill (deputy leader of Vanguard), Stanley McMaster (Westminster MP for East Belfast), Willie Orr, Brian Smyth of the Young Unionist Council, and Colonel James Cunningham, a hardline Unionist grandee. Although Willie Long disapproved of Vanguard, he did not support us, on the ground that membership of a political party was essentially a personal matter, to be decided by the individual who, if he found himself in violent disagreement with the policies of the party, should decide whether to remain or not.

After two hours, a resolution was put that the original motion be dropped without a vote and that the next business on the agenda be proceeded with. This resolution was carried by 121 votes. There were a large number of abstentions. There was then a bizarre alliance of supporters of both sides to the debate, including Stratton Mills, Bill Craig, Roy Bradford, Captain Austin Ardill, John Taylor, Martin Smyth and myself, arguing that the original motion moved by Stratton Mills and seconded by myself be put to a vote. Between us, however, we could raise only 62 votes. In all, 128 delegates followed the advice of Brian Faulkner, the party leader, to avoid any sort of confrontation, and voted down the motion. The committee decided to pass on to new business, whereupon thirty or forty delegates, including Stratton and myself, walked out of the hall. The meeting and its procedures had been a shambles.

Speaking at the meeting Brian Faulkner ruled out any question of UDI or negotiated independence and gave Vanguard supporters no comfort about his policy. He claimed afterwards that there were no links between the two bodies that could be cut and that the acceptance of a resolution to leave the dual membership issue and proceed with other business had been a 'great victory of the centre of the party'. It was not – it was a great fudge. The initial motion was liberal Unionist, seeking to halt the spreading influence of Vanguard which we saw was damaging the Unionist Party's credibility. The outcome was a rebuff to Stratton and myself, and a diminution of our standing within the party.

A few days later Stratton resigned from the Unionist Party. It was widely believed that I would follow suit. His decision was a serious set-back to me as liberal forces within the party were already thin on the ground. I received a number of letters from people concerned about my political soul. They suggested that I either help form a new, moderate unionist party or join the Alliance Party where I could be washed squeaky clean. Some concluded by asking how long I thought I could remain with the Official Unionists (UUP). I felt, however, that neither the Alliance Party nor any other party could attract much independent support in the Protestant community and so I resigned myself to work from within. My future in the party would be decided by the attitude of members of the UUP to the British government's White Paper, to be published in the New Year, on the political reconstruction of Northern Ireland.

The White Paper was published on 20 March 1973, and controversy soon raged over it. The White Paper called for a Northern Ireland Assembly of seventy-eight members elected by proportional representation from multi-member constituencies, and it quickly became clear, first, that under the proposals the SDLP would inevitably be involved in a future Executive and, second, that the Assembly would be a downgraded Stormont.

The White Paper said the British government's view was that 'the Executive itself can no longer be based solely upon any single party if that party draws its support and its elected representatives from only one section of the community'. That was bad enough for some, but even more startling were the proposals for relations with the Republic of Ireland. The White Paper concluded that it was 'clearly desirable that any new arrangements for Northern Ireland should, whilst meeting the wishes of Northern Ireland and Great Britain, be so far as possible acceptable to and acceptable by the Republic of Ireland'.

Areas of mutual interest between North and South were identified, such as tourism, regional development, electricity, and transport, where a Council of Ireland might prove useful. The White Paper outlined the 'Irish dimension' as including talks between the British government, the government of the Republic and representatives from Northern Ireland at a conference to discuss the acceptance of the existing status of Northern Ireland, and the provision of a firm basis for concerted action against terrorism. Responsibilities to be devolved to an Executive would include social security, education, industry, agriculture and planning. It was hoped that the control of security might be handed over to the Executive at an unspecified date in the future.

Clearly Stormont had gone for good. The old order must yield to something new and acceptable to the people of Northern Ireland involving both communities at the highest level. My private reaction was that the White Paper was an offer that held much promise for a new deal for everyone; moreover, with Westminster calling the tune, it was the only way of getting back a devolved administration. As a Unionist who preferred to live within the UK, and under its sole ultimate jurisdiction, I was considerably less sanguine about the implications of an 'Irish dimension'. But the White Paper would give us what we had sought since the suspension of Stormont — an elected assembly of the people of Northern Ireland. It indicated that the full resources of the government of the UK would be deployed in our support. And it assured us that under no circumstances would we cease to be citizens of the UK, unless it was by the expressed will of the majority of people in Northern Ireland. It would give us power to legislate about a wide range of activities, and the security forces of the UK would remain to assist in the preservation of law and order for as long as they were needed.

We were being offered a last chance to save ourselves from ourselves.

What we needed was a broader vision to realise that, for the foreseeable future, we needed to come to terms with the radical theory and difficult practice of consensus government. A broad spectrum of representatives of ability could contribute to the exercise of government, given understanding and willingness in the interest of the common good.

The British government went ahead with its White Paper proposals for an Assembly elected by proportional representation, and power-sharing between the parties as an alternative to majority government. Unionists were sharply divided on the document, but the SDLP and Alliance gave it a general welcome. The strategy and details of the Irish dimension were left to the Sunningdale Conference to be held later.

By the run-up to the June Assembly elections the split in the Unionist Party had become formalised into a division between 'pledged' or 'Official Unionist' candidates supporting the Faulkner line, and 'unpledged' or 'Unionist' candidates those against the White Paper. A loyalist coalition was formed outside the party consisting of Ian Paisley's Democratic Unionist Party and Bill Craig's Vanguard Party.

I was confronted by the cold reality that my political prospects were not good, to say the least. The signs were ominous for any progress on the White Paper with the odds so heavily stacked against the 'pledged' Unionists. Yet again I had to halt at my own personal crossroads. I knew I had much personal support in my erstwhile constituency and from Brian Faulkner who encouraged me to stay on. Should I stand for election? Or should I drop out, like so many others, and give my undivided attention to practice at the Bar, with which I had been trying to keep in contact? I felt a paramount duty to our children who had reached the expensive stage, which would only get more expensive until they were launched in life.

But to choose to bow out of politics at that point would have been to abandon the field to the other side. I could not in all conscience do this, nor would pride or self-respect allow me to. So I decided to run with the ball and applied for an Official Unionist nomination for the six-member constituency of South Belfast (the election would be under a proportional representation system known as 'single transferable vote'). The Faulknerite line was clearly under threat of becoming the minority view in the unionist community. As I had so recently vehemently supported it I felt it was touch and go whether I would win selection as a Unionist candidate. But I did – just – at a South Belfast Unionist selection committee meeting held at the Stranmillis Hall on 16 May – along with Herbie Kirk (former minister of finance), Reggie Magee (a consultant obstetrician and gynaecologist and a newcomer to active politics) and ex-senator Nelson Elder.

The Northern Ireland Assembly election was held on 23 June 1973 – a day of brilliant summer sunshine. The results, though ambiguous enough not to hamper seriously the progress or dampen the determination of the moderate Unionists, were clearly a sign of worse to come, when I got down to analysing them after the satisfaction at my own success had worn off.

Of the moderate Unionists, Brian Faulkner topped the poll (with double the quota) in South Down, his fiefdom. I topped the poll in South Belfast which had an electorate of 75,990, of which 70.6 per cent turned out to vote. But other moderates did not do so well. The few successes were in middle-class areas (where the Alliance Party also did well), or drew on personal followings, or a mixture of both. Of the 32 Unionist Party members of the new Assembly, only 24 were 'pledged' Unionists in favour of powersharing. In all 18 'loyalists' were elected, 8 Alliance, 19 SDLP and 1 Northern Ireland Labour Party. Although the powersharing parties together had a sizeable majority (50 to 28), the split in the Unionist Party would turn out to be a crucial factor. The loyalist coalition, a close political bloc, did ominously well against the liberal Unionists, whereas the SDLP completely wiped out republican competitors on their side.

On Friday, 5 October 1973, representatives of Alliance, pro-Assembly Unionists and SDLP Assembly members met in the old Cabinet Room in Stormont Castle for the first formal interparty talks on the formation of a powersharing Executive. I had been included by Brian Faulkner in the Unionist deputation of six. We knew that we were by no means representative of grassroots Protestant opinion. I said to Brian as we walked up the steps of Stormont Castle that morning that someone had to do what we were about to do, but that it could be the end of a political career for all of us.

The negotiations at Stormont under Willie Whitelaw during October and November were an exhilarating if exhausting experience. Real progress was being made in Northern Ireland for the first time. Yet we knew that Protestant opposition was growing. Sticking points were over policing, detention and the Council of Ireland. It was the last that worried us most, as around it was coalescing a formidable loyalist opposition. A Council of Ireland, an institution regarded by many Protestants as an external threat and as specifically designed ultimately to bring about a united Ireland, was something we could not sell. Powersharing appeared to be a lesser concern.

It is at least arguable that powersharing on its own could have been sold to the Protestant majority. But the SDLP and the Dublin government had been increasingly taking over the Council of Ireland idea. It was manifestly clear that most Dublin and SDLP politicians regarded the discussions on constitutional reform in Northern Ireland as an opportunity to extract the greatest possible concessions from the Unionists through pressure from Westminster. They believed London could be persuaded to use the proposals ultimately to rid Britain of the whole problem via Irish unification.

The police issue was connected, as there had been a suggestion (advanced by John Hume particularly) that the Northern Ireland Police Authority should be controlled by the Council of Ireland. Liberal Unionists like myself felt there was a possibility of selling the Council of Ireland if it could be seen as a means of improving the security situation through North–South cooperation on extradition and law and order.

Meanwhile, on 25 October, a Vanguard Assembly member, Glenn Barr, made what was considered the first 'Ulster nationalist' speech at Stormont. He said:

I have no intention of remaining a British citizen at any price. The price being put on British citizenship under the Constitution Act is too much to bear. It has got to be borne in mind that Ulstermen have more pride than to accept a White Paper that has been thrown across the Irish Sea at them. . . . An Ulsterman's first allegiance must be the state of Ulster. True Ulstermen must reject anything which in any way indicates that Ulster is going to be put into a United Ireland. True Ulstermen must therefore reject the Constitution Act. Let it be put on record that I stand here as an Ulster Nationalist.

Barr reflected the instinct of the strong nationalist element in Ulster Protestants that their constitutional status was embedded in a separate culture and history (one utterly distinct from both Irish republican and British counterparts).

Despite the alarms, and through the skill of Willie Whitelaw, agreement was finally reached on the formation of an Executive. I remember vividly, at the last meeting of the negotiations on 22 November, seeing tears coursing down Willie's face at the moment he knew his mission had been accomplished. There had been days of tense wrangling in the numbers game, when Gerry Fitt was adamant that the SDLP would only accept an Executive comprising 5 Unionists, 5 SDLP and 2 Alliance. Brian Faulkner held out for 7 Unionists or nothing, pointing out that any seats at all in government was an advance for Alliance and the SDLP. He stated his absolute commitment to a Unionist majority on the Executive. Complete breakdown on the issue was never far away. But this was averted when the composition of the Executive was ultimately agreed to be Unionists 6, the SDLP 4, and the Alliance Party 1 (Fitt had said previously that a 6:4:1 Executive was an insult to the SDLP). The SDLP and Alliance, however, got two non-voting portfolios, that is, two positions outside the Executive but part of the administration. Through the compromise on numbers a majority of Unionists, albeit of only one, was secured at the same time as the involvement of a number of active SDLP politicians in government was assured. But we had succeeded in reaching an agreement knowing that, outside, there were politicians and terrorists who together hoped to see us fail.

The formation of an Executive was announced at lunchtime on 22 November 1973. It was all over bar the allocation of portfolios.

There had been a hiccup earlier in the morning on the 'numbers game'. Paddy Devlin rang up Peter McLachlan, an Assembly member and one of Faulkner's closest advisers, alerting him to the possibility of a crisis, which may have had something to do with Paddy's coveting of the health and social services portfolio. I, for my part, was fearful of being left out in the cold, in spite of having already held a cabinet post and taken the risk of pursuing an unpopular liberal line. I could see myself being marginalised on the back benches, out of a sense of loyalty endeavouring to keep alive an interest in politics whilst trying to resuscitate an ailing practice at the Bar. My future was very much in the balance. It would be a personal humiliation and a very bitter pill if I were not to be found a place in the Executive.

On the day after the numbers controversy had been decided, the media speculated on who would get what portfolio in the Executive. I was not among those singled out. Sick with fear and apprehension I nervously rang up Brian's home at Seaforde to press my claim for inclusion in the team. He was in London. But I need not have worried for on the next day he rang me at home to ask, 'How would you like to have something to do with schools?' I was delighted to know that I was to be appointed minister for education. I had dug deep into my reserves of emotional energy for some time. Now it all seemed to have been worthwhile.

The Executive met at Stormont in the former prime minister's room. On a wall a portrait of Sir Henry Wilson, Chief of the Imperial General Staff, an Irish Unionist and violently anti-republican, who was assassinated by the IRA in a London street in 1922, reminded us (if we needed reminding) of our troubled history. My seat at the table was beside John Hume. I found his cold certainties, and the goals and imperatives that drove him, not altogether comfortable, even intimidating. I have to say I felt more at ease with the earnest Austin Currie opposite – a man of ability, commitment and considerable courage – and with Gerry Fitt and Paddy Devlin. With the jaunty, cheerful Gerry, what you saw was what you got. Paddy Devlin's individualistic and irreverent no-nonsense approach was highly entertaining. He did not suffer fools gladly, and in the short time available to him was to become a most effective minister of health and social services.

In the late afternoon of 5 December 1973 I was sitting on a front bench near the door of the debating chamber when Ian Paisley arose on a spurious point of order during a renewed Assembly debate on unemployment. According to him, this was a matter of much more immediate importance than the imminent Sunningdale Conference to which he claimed he and the loyalists had not been invited (in fact, an invitation to attend the first session had been handed to him in the middle of the debate).

I was excited at the prospect of taking part in what was to be one of the most historic conferences in the history of Ireland and was preoccupied as I waited to join my colleagues for the flight to London. Out of the corner of my eye I noticed two burly figures, Douglas Hutchinson and Charlie Poots, members of Vanguard and the Democratic Unionist Party, coming purposefully towards me. Earlier that day in an empty corridor outside, one of them had obstructed and jostled me. Now, catching hold of my arms they jerked me off the bench and to my feet and proceeded to tighten my tie as if to strangle me. This was no time for turning the other cheek and I was strong enough to make them stagger and thus to free myself. They then directed their attentions to Peter McLachlan and Herbie Kirk whom they violently assaulted. The damage to my jacket – one sleeve ripped, lining hanging loose, and the loss of a few buttons – was nothing to my fury at the indignity; it was this fury that provided me with the strength to see them off.

Paisley's spurious point of order had been a prearranged signal for the nonsense that followed. An anti-powersharing group composed of Harry West's Unionists, Ian Paisley's Democratic Unionists, Bill Craig's Vanguard, and Hugh Smyth's Independent Unionists had met earlier that day to plan a physical assault in the chamber on the Faulkner Unionists as a publicity stunt. Those who participated were told who they were to make for when the signal was given. I was to receive the attention of Hutchinson and Poots.

One might have thought that scenes like this would have gone some way towards discrediting the loyalist faction in the eyes of the public. Not a bit of it. That this was not the case was an indication of the bitterness felt by many Protestants towards the Sunningdale initiative.

A short time later in the Cabinet Room, where we were foregathering prior to being bussed to Aldergrove airport, Roy Bradford, who had not been in the debating chamber at the time of the incident, pointed an accusing finger at the angry, tattered figure standing before him, 'McIvor,' he said, 'you would do anything for publicity!' A response more solicitous as to my welfare came from the distinguished and courteous Brigadier Joseph Callendar Broadhurst, who was a strong supporter of Brian Faulkner. That evening he rang Jill, who had not seen the media coverage of the incident, kindly enquiring, 'And how is the dear chap?' Jill replied that, as far as she knew, I was well and at Sunningdale.

The journey to London that dark wet night was strangely unreal. For security reasons the bus journey from London to Sunningdale was circuitous and prolonged, allowing Unionists and nationalists time to indulge in provocative party songs and the freedom of friendly banter. I would say that I have a generally good sense of humour, but it was sorely tested that evening at Sunningdale when BBC1 television news carried an interview with Paisley about the violent scenes in the Assembly, in which he claimed, 'McIvor struck the first blow.'

The Sunningdale Conference continued until 9 December; it was the first conference since 1925 at which the heads of government of Britain and both parts of Ireland were present. The main objective was to put flesh on the ideas for an 'Irish dimension'. On the evening of 6 December, Ted Heath held a dinner for the delegates at 10 Downing Street. Amongst those present were Sir Alex Douglas-Home (the foreign secretary), Peter Rawlinson (the attorney-general) and Francis Pym (the new secretary of state for Northern Ireland). The Irish negotiating team included the taoiseach, Liam Cosgrave, Brendan Corish, leader of the Irish Labour Party, the minister of foreign affairs Garret FitzGerald, and Conor Cruise O'Brien, minister for posts and telegraphs.

Powersharing and a Council of Ireland were to prove a fatal mixture. Throughout the course of the conference I felt it was all a pretty hopeless exercise. I shall never forget the long night sessions when we Unionists waited for Brian Faulkner to come down from the upstairs room where a communiqué was being drafted by the heads of government, leaders of parties, and civil servants. He would come down every now and again with a piece of paper on which was the latest idea. 'What about this, boys?' he would say. 'No, Brian!' we would reply. 'We couldn't possibly get away with that.'

At 4 o'clock one morning, the stiff and moody Ted Heath,

accompanied by Frank Cooper, the permanent undersecretary of the Northern Ireland Office, came down to our room. For a moment the prime minister stared at us, fixing each with his pale blue eyes. Then: 'You people want everything,' he exploded. 'There is no satisfying you!' We protested that there was a large disaffected population waiting for us back home who were opposed to us being there in the first place, and that we must somehow get them on board. There was no way we could do so if the present wording of the communiqué on the Council of Ireland remained as it was. On his way out of the room back to the drafting upstairs, Heath turned round, hand still on the door, and grinned in our direction, shoulders characteristically heaving. Frank Cooper winked as he left. What this was meant to signify was not clear. One would like to think that it was an analeptic gesture to make up in small measure for the hard time he had been giving us, saying perhaps: You're all awful, but I admire you!

The problem was that the Unionist contingent was not prepared to agree to a Council of Ireland unless it was solely an advisory body on harmonising functions of a cross-border nature such as tourism, transport, agriculture and electricity. On the other hand the general approach of the SDLP, notably John Hume, was to achieve all-Ireland institutions that would produce the dynamic that could lead ultimately to an agreed single state of Ireland.

Extradition was an issue on which it became quickly and abundantly clear that no ground would be given. John Baxter, Harry Calvert and myself, the three lawyers, were tasked to represent the Unionists at the technical discussions on fugitive offenders, the extradition issue and related matters such as common law enforcement, political offences and international legal conventions. I strongly urged the case for extradition, citing the general trend of security policy in Europe. The Irish contingent would not yield, and there was no adequate support from the British side, mainly because Britain had not a leg to stand on. Since the time when Marx and Engels lived in Britain the British have tolerated, even encouraged, those with anti-establishment views to settle in Britain, where their offence or offences were 'political' – defined by John Stuart Mill as 'any offence committed in the course of civil war, insurrection or commotion'. This accepted principle was the subject of legislation in the 1870 British Extradition Act which declared: 'No person is to be surrendered if his offence is one of a political character.'

In line with this, and from the South's point of view, the question was how the Republic should regard members of the IRA and similar organisations who fled south. Most people regarded the IRA as different from ordinary criminals inasmuch as some thought them better and some worse. Protestants, of course, believed the IRA to be worse than ordinary criminals. At that time in Northern Ireland the authorities had brought a series of requests for the return of IRA suspects who had fled south. None was successful. Declan Costello, the Irish attorney-general, was suggesting a common court, nominated by and legislated for by the Council of Ireland. There was a total impasse – no meeting of minds.

On the day we abandoned the discussions, Peter Rawlinson came looking for me to tell me that somebody had come up with the bright idea that we should consider using existing powers under an old Act of Parliament whereby an offender who had committed a crime in Northern Ireland and had fled to the Republic could be arrested and tried for that offence in the Republic; one of the difficulties, of course, would be persuading witnesses from the North to testify in the South's courts. This was not what we were looking for and was hardly a concession likely to impress the hardline opposition back home – nor was another proposal: to establish a joint law commission. We needed action on extradition, and now. On the other hand, for the Irish government to accede to extradition would have meant that support for the Executive in the Republic would have crumbled.

It was at this point that the Unionists could see the futility of it all. We had gained nothing. I would have left if we could have been sure that powersharing would survive. But politically the Executive couldn't go ahead without agreement at Sunningdale. The suggested Council of Ireland with its three tiers (meetings between Belfast and Dublin ministers, a joint parliamentary body, and a permanent secretariat) was bad enough, but to add to it the refusal to permit extradition of terrorist suspects – something that might have strengthened the Unionist position – ruined any chance that we could sell the powersharing experiment. Early next morning, following a long negotiating session through the night, I shared these anxieties with Brian, and he suggested we take a turn round the gardens for a breath of fresh air. We had had little sleep over the past thirty hours.

The day was bright and crisp, with frost sparkling from the paths as we slowly walked about taking stock. Suddenly we came upon the taoiseach and Conor Cruise O'Brien similarly engaged. We asked them how they saw the situation. Both of them sadly agreed that, the way things were looking, we Unionists were not going to be able to sell Sunningdale to our people at home.

In his book *Ancestral Voices*, Conor Cruise O'Brien was subsequently to write that he warned the Dublin government in cabinet against emphasis on the Council of Ireland; he also warned that the important thing was to secure the cross-community Executive, and that by piling on a lot of surplus symbolism, we were in danger of capsizing the essential – the powersharing Executive. He criticised Garret FitzGerald – briefed by John Hume – for telling the British cabinet that this danger did not exist and that the Unionist community would accept Sunningdale, Council of Ireland and all.

Either deliberately ignoring or being unaware of Unionist fears to the point of arrogance, Hume's was to be a fatal misjudgement. He alone amongst the SDLP had pushed hard for a Council of Ireland that would not be some anodyne, insignificant institution concerned to assuage fears in the North, but instead the full works: a high-profile construction – the 'bridge too far'. Hume was a close friend of Garret FitzGerald, and the two families had spent part of August 1973 on holiday together in Donegal when, presumably, this strategy was discussed.

It was Hume who did the television interviews from which the Protestants of Northern Ireland learned the details of powersharing and the Council of Ireland. Roy Bradford, our pit canary at Sunningdale, sensitive to the slightest whiff of danger to our position, filled that role for the Unionists. After Brian's signature to the agreement had been secured, those watching television in Northern Ireland could detect from Hume's triumphalism that he knew he had won.

To John Hume, the most significant and visionary nationalist politician of his generation, a united Ireland is a romantic eternal absolute. His reasoning is deductive. First set out your goal and from that standpoint direct all arguments towards achieving it. He does not believe in starting with the established facts and realities and then working slowly upwards towards the desired result. At that time he never understood the genuine historic fears and sensitivities of the unionists, however much these understandably irritated him. Nor did he want to. He finds it hard to empathise with unionists. In unionist eyes he wore the nationalist mantle of odium as did Daniel O'Connell in the 1820s, although O'Connell deserved the reproach less. If he ever addressed the fears of unionists it was to say blandly that they had nothing to fear, that they had no need to keep pressing the British government to reiterate its policy that the status of Northern Ireland would remain as it was unless there was a majority in favour of change. The unionists, he argues, should stand on their own feet and see how they could come to live in peace and harmony with the 'people of this island'. This is a splendid piece of hypocrisy considering the pan-nationalist front he has established in Dublin and amongst the Irish-American lobby to bolster his own political position. To redress the balance, unionism would have had a much more difficult task: to cultivate in the cause of unionism the Scots/Irish diaspora in the United States which has long since become absorbed in the mainstream of Anglo-Saxon America.

This kind of extraordinary insensitivity was hardly likely to endear Hume to unionists, and it was not surprising that he was deeply distrusted by the unionist community at large. He was grim and unbending in negotiation. I have never been able to detect any sense of humour in John. But then I was never close to him, and his friends may say differently.

His part in the Sunningdale Agreement spelt disaster for the survival of powersharing. To me he was the man who, at Sunningdale, blew out the light at the end of the tunnel. His insistence on the promise of a Council of Ireland, which he must surely have anticipated would arouse fierce opposition amongst the majority of Protestants, wrecked the prospects of an otherwise excellent and hopeful powersharing arrangement.

Given time, the sectarian issue might well have given way to social/economic issues and, with the building up of trust, the Executive might well have succeeded in accommodating the arch-Tory tendencies of

Roy Bradford and the fundamental socialism of Paddy Devlin and Gerry Fitt in the interests of keeping the show on the road. John Hume, as minister of commerce, could have developed his American interests to bring investment into Northern Ireland. I do not believe, however, he would have been comfortable with a political role that confined him to Northern Ireland. His scene is obviously on the world stage.

His heart was never to be in the powersharing Executive. His interest in it was that it might prove to be an agent for the eventual reunification of Ireland. And yet he has courageously done much to promote peace in Northern Ireland within the context of his own nationalist aspirations, and has been a force in compelling Unionists, and rightly so, to engage in dialogue with their arch enemy, Sinn Féin.

7

THE FALL OF THE EXECUTIVE

A BITTERLY COLD AND MISERABLE FLIGHT back to Belfast on 19 December in an unheated RAF aircraft was in keeping with the depression I felt. The outlook was gloomy. However, I tried hard to put the traditional family pleasures of Christmas between myself and the opening of the Assembly in the New Year.

The Executive took office on New Year's Day 1974. A few days later, on 4 January, the lines were drawn when, at an Ulster Unionist Council (the governing body of the party), Brian Faulkner was defeated on a crucial vote: the UUC rejected the 'proposed all-Ireland Council settlement' by 427 votes to 374. In the wake of this defeat, he resigned as Unionist Party leader, spelling the death knell of the Executive.

Trouble began on 21 January. The bells had rung for the beginning of the sitting when it was discovered that Ian Paisley, John Taylor, the Reverend William Beattie, Douglas Hutchinson, Ernest Baird, Hugh Smyth and the absurd, eccentric Professor Kennedy Lindsay (who for one Assembly debate had donned a Nigerian ceremonial robe to make a point) were occupying the government front bench. Under the rules of the Assembly this area was reserved for the Executive. So-called loyalists shouted and ran about the chamber, the mace was passed from hand to hand, and Kennedy Lindsay jumped on the clerk's table shouting, 'We have cleared the money changers from the temple.'

Brian Faulkner, grim and with arms folded, was standing just inside the entrance to the chamber along with other members of the Executive. Kennedy Lindsay at one stage tried unsuccessfully to attach himself to the front bench with a long black chain. I moved over beside Brian when I thought the situation was becoming increasingly menacing. If anyone laid a finger on him he would have to deal with me first! But I am sure he could have looked after himself. I saw Lindsay come towards him and spit in his face. We were all subjected to verbal abuse including being labelled 'traitors' and 'murderers'.

Four hundred police were on duty at the Assembly. Outside the building, troops and armoured vehicles were thick on the ground. A large force of police moved into the building and carried out the troublemakers. Ian Paisley was carried out feet first, without a struggle. His deputy, William Beattie, walked out. Both wrestled with police outside the door as they attempted to get back in. We finally managed to take our places on the front bench seventy minutes after the Assembly's scheduled starting time. These disgraceful scenes were shown on local and national television that evening.

The Executive put out a statement which said amongst other things:

Today's events point up sharply the choice which the people of Northern Ireland have before them. We in the Executive spoke yesterday in our statement of aims, in terms of jobs, houses, schools and factories. Others replied today in their own terms: shouts, threats, abuse and utter disrespect for anyone else's right to speak. The political struggle in Northern Ireland is in reality about whether we as a community cherish free institutions sufficiently to uphold them. There were present in the Assembly today members who neither support the Executive nor played any part in the disgraceful and disorderly proceedings. We believe that amongst them are some who share our dismay and disgust. If this is so, their voices should be heard. In such circumstances as these, silence is not enough.

Some opponents of the Executive obviously did not accept that there was any distinction between verbal and physical opposition, but a significant percentage did. At least one-third of the opposition took no part in the violence.

It was a bad start for the Executive. It was never able to get going as rising feeling in the Protestant community against Sunningdale was fuelled by external events beyond its control. For example, there was the Boland case. Kevin Boland, a minister in the previous Fianna Fáil government in Dublin who had resigned at the time of a gun-running scandal, challenged the Sunningdale Agreement in the Republic's courts. He argued that the articles claiming Northern Ireland as part of the national territory in the Irish Constitution could not be reconciled with those sections of the Sunningdale communiqué that expressed recognition of the status of Northern Ireland. Both the Dublin government and Faulkner were put in a very awkward position and, though a ruling in favour of the Irish government followed, even an unsuccessful appeal continued to fuel loyalist reaction.

Then there followed the February Westminster elections called by Heath, the results of which were an unmitigated disaster for the liberal Unionists, and effectively destroyed the legitimacy of the Executive in the eyes of the Protestant community. Under the beguiling slogan 'Dublin is only a Sunningdale away', the loyalist coalition took eleven of the twelve seats, with Gerry Fitt, the deputy chief of the Executive, retaining his West Belfast seat for the SDLP. The election was the fourth time Northern Ireland voters had gone to the polls in less than a year. The reason for its being called was mainly the miners' strike in Britain, but unfortunately the only issue in Northern Ireland was the Sunningdale Agreement, and the Executive parties (Unionist, SDLP and Alliance) were seriously embarrassed by having to defend a system that had barely got off the ground.

Merlyn Rees became the secretary of state for Northern Ireland under the new Labour administration of Harold Wilson. I was invited to join Brian Faulkner and Rees for lunch at the Stormont Hotel shortly after the latter's arrival in Northern Ireland to update him on the current situation. It was plain that the Executive had made little or no impact on the population so far. The only thing I took away from the lunch was Rees's suggestion that planting trees in the centre of Belfast might be a useful symbolic gesture to show the Executive was in business. I think he really meant it. Well meaning but naïve.

Mindful of the rising opposition to us, the Unionists in the Executive began to back-pedal. We tried to renegotiate the Council of Ireland with the SDLP by stringing out its implementation.

On 27 April I had the opportunity to promote my views in the South. I was one of the guest speakers at the Comhchomhairle Chorcaí annual seminar at the Silver Springs Hotel outside Cork. Entitled 'Can the Irish traditions be reconciled?', the seminar was chaired by the former Fianna Fáil taoiseach, Jack Lynch.

I began my speech by pointing out that the Northern Ireland Constitution Act of 1973 enshrined for the people of Northern Ireland the right to self-determination, a right underwritten at Sunningdale and fundamental to the administration of power in the North. This must be the cornerstone of any arrangements for cooperation between North and South, I said. A Council of Ireland based on the view that it was a step towards the unification of Ireland rather than a forum to foster understanding and development for the benefit of people north and south could not succeed. Anyone who presented the council purely as a tool for unification would immediately alienate a substantial body of opinion in Northern Ireland and make it extremely difficult for the elected representatives of that opinion to participate properly. Equally, those who refused to recognise that it was possible to establish machinery for formal cooperation between north and south that would be in the interests of both, would be refusing to recognise the realities of the situation by adopting a reactionary attitude in the interests of no one.

I said I believed it to be perfectly feasible for northern Protestants (wedded to the existing links with Britain) to sit down with their Catholic neighbours of the South or the North (who equally firmly believed in the ultimate unification of Ireland) in meaningful dialogue to mutual benefit. A Council of Ireland that demanded of either the abandonment of basic and sincerely held beliefs would be totally unrealistic. This had to be explained to the electorates in both parts of the island.

A successful Council of Ireland must therefore be built on the understanding by all sides of the differing aspirations of others, on mutual respect and on absolute trust. The Sunningdale Agreement would stand or fall on maintaining that respect and trust. We in the North would be looking to the South for support in the defeat of terrorism and in the isolation and elimination of extremism. The South, in turn, would be looking to the North for a similar elimination of extremism and for a more extroverted and less defensive approach to our relations. For every extremist that either side could isolate and leave helpless, one would disappear on the other side. Extremists fed on each other and justified each other. I believed that a determined all-Ireland effort to eliminate extremism in whatever form would be a great contribution to the quest for lasting peace. My speech was received with polite applause, whilst afterwards individuals were welcoming and hopeful that our visit might be a step forward.

Meanwhile, Anglo-Irish talks in London had led to the distinct impression that Sunningdale was to be ratified in May. What in fact was needed then was a shelving of the issue for a few months until things cooled down. Against this background, in March 1974 the IRA moved onto the offensive again, making common cause with Ian Paisley in wrecking the attempt at political compromise. Belfast, Bangor and Lisburn were blitzed over two days at the end of March. I visited Lisburn with Stanley Orme, then minister of state. His united-Ireland aspirations were well known. The affront offered to shopkeepers, standing amongst the rubble of their shops in Bow Street, by his presence was palpable. I was acutely embarrassed as I walked down the street alongside him.

In April, a 500-pound bomb exploded in Belfast's main shopping area. Britain's reaction was to legalise both Sinn Féin and the Ulster Volunteer Force (the UVF, the Protestant paramilitary force which in the 1960s had attempted to destabilise O'Neill's reforms by several attacks on the Silent Valley reservoir, Belfast's main water supply, and had subsequently mounted attacks on Catholics, including the bombing of McGurk's bar). It was an extraordinary response which also promised phased releases of detainees and a scheme for assigning them after release to 'sponsors' who would keep them on the straight and narrow. Dubbed 'take a terrorist home to tea', the response was incredibly naïve and tactless of the new Labour administration. But rapidly this softly, softly approach ran up against the raw facts of the situation, as the IRA was encouraged to carry out further bombings. Belfast was paralysed by bombs that cut off all major roads. The shopping centre of the historic city of Armagh was burnt out.

As minister of education I had to handle a number of sensitive and complex issues, especially the challenge to the eleven-plus system, the reform of teacher education, and the education of Catholics and Protestant children side by side in the same schools (integrated education), the oldest sore spot of them all. I had come to office at a time when the relationship between the Department of Education and the new Area Education and Library Boards had yet to be worked out in detail.

What would be the balance of power between the centre and the periphery? How would voluntary schools fare under the new system? In normal times these problems would have taxed the capacity of any minister of education but with the administration in terminal decline and with the Executive embattled on every side, the gloomy futility of it all was totally dispiriting. I was also entrusted with 'a detailed investigation of the role of education in the promotion of community harmony, and the development of pilot experiments, after consultation with interested parties, in integrated education'.

In December 1973, Sir John Wolfenden (later Lord Wolfenden) had accepted an invitation by the Joseph Rowntree Memorial Trust to conduct a study of ways in which the educational system might help to create better understanding between the two communities in Northern Ireland. In early 1974, I discussed our education system with him in

London in the light of that assignment. He subsequently produced a report, which was never published. The Rowntree Trust refused to release it although Lord Wolfenden had no objection. Why it was suspended I never knew. I wondered had it recommended some form of integrated schooling. Three opinion polls over the previous ten years had shown a majority of Catholics and Protestants to be in favour of shared schooling for their children. Many parents longed to see integrated education but felt they were powerless against the church and state authorities.

Northern Ireland had the highest degree of religious segregation in its school population in the Christian world. Those who would seek to maintain this division had much to answer for. And so when my permanent secretary, Arthur Brooke, came into my room one morning and asked me what my instructions were on the role of education in the promotion of community harmony, I asked him to have his civil servants investigate and report to me on the possibilities of shared schools within the system.

Initially the civil servants refused to take this on. Bureaucratic reaction to changing the education system in such a radical way was not unexpected. As Maurice Hayes observes in his memoir *Minority Verdict*:

> One of the effects of single-party government for seventy years, and a Civil Service that reflected the values and ethos of the dominant party, was a lack of challenge, a lack of intellectual vigour, a willingness to accept traditional attitudes and procedures as immutable. . . . [in part] because of what association with doomed policy initiatives would do to official careers.

But Arthur Brooke made it clear to his senior officials that this was an order which must be carried out. In late April 1974, furnished with a draft Shared School Plan, I was ready to enter the minefield.

I knew that the Executive would not last much longer, but it was some time before I could get my proposals put on the agenda. I had been carrying the document around for days in my slim official EIIR briefcase, hoping to slip it in at some meeting of the Executive. All of these meetings, however, were fraught with anxieties about the worsening situation outside. My plan eventually made the agenda in late April 1974; there was no opportunity or indeed time to do any lobbying with the members of the Executive beforehand. I proposed to my colleagues the establishment of a third type of school, in addition to the existing state controlled schools (Protestant) and the maintained schools (Catholic). This was to be a 'shared school', available to Catholic and Protestant parents alike who wished to see their children educated together.

I had already written to the leaders of the main churches explaining briefly the scheme. But I realised that if I were to enter into consultation with the churches, the matter would never get beyond the restatement of positions, or at most statements welcoming the scheme in principle. We could never hope for anything concrete to emerge in the light of a historical outright resistance to integration or, in the case of some churches, timid acceptance that something must be done about it in the future, but not just now (what about integrating the shipyard first? or housing?). A few minutes before going into that meeting of the Executive, I had received a telephone message from Cardinal Conway warning me not to interfere with the schools. I mentioned this to Faulkner who briefly told me to carry on, I would have his support.

The Executive unanimously approved and welcomed the 'shared schools' plan with the exception of John Hume who was less than enthusiastic. I came away with authority to get on with it. This was an occasion, ministers decided, when it should be seen that we were giving a lead to the community without seeking the imprimatur of the clergy or the views of any other section of society.

On that same day, the leaders of the main churches were meeting together in ecumenical fellowship at an hotel at Ballymascanlon, outside Dundalk. They were unprepared for the announcement of the plan on the evening news – even though they must have known from my letters to them what was in my mind. It seems they had been discussing everything that might help to bring the communities together, except integrated education. When interviewed, Cardinal Conway said that, as he had not discussed the idea with the minister, he could not comment on it – he wasn't quite sure what was in the minister's mind. The Presbyterian and Church of Ireland leaders gave the proposal a mild welcome, whilst the Methodists warmly welcomed it.

I provided details in a statement to the Assembly on 30 April. First I declared my basic belief that mixing schoolchildren would contribute to the reduction of community tension in Northern Ireland. Although I realised that the churches would have some hesitation, I asked them earnestly to consider the very special needs of Northern Ireland and to join the Executive in a constructive approach to meeting these needs. I acknowledged that one of the grounds for hesitation by the churches was an understandable anxiety about the religious upbringing of their children in schools not under their own management. The management of schools was, however, a matter about which we in the Assembly could do something.

Specifically, I suggested that the law should be changed to facilitate another class of school. In the management of the new shared schools, the two groups of churches would be equally involved. We thought that if the main groups of churches were to be involved together in the management of a school they would between them have sufficient goodwill to agree what should be done, and to make arrangements that would enable the children in the shared school to be suitably instructed in the tenets of their own church. A start was to be made with the provision of integrated nursery schools. Funding of £13 million would be made available for this purpose over the following ten years. I advised the Assembly that I thought it likely that in the autumn I would have to suggest some technical amendments to the education legislation.

I said I saw this statement as a deliberately timid entry into the field, knowing I would have to tread carefully. I did not see a wholesale switch to shared status, but hoped that over the years there would be a gradual growth which would embrace existing schools as well as new ones. For me, as I stood addressing the Assembly on that day, it seemed a mischievously wicked dream. I tried to put to the back of my mind the realisation that the Assembly could not last much longer.

My plan received a predictably mixed reaction. My fellow Unionist John Taylor, a Presbyterian elder, welcomed it saying, 'I believe that any suggestion about this subject, whether from the discredited Executive or otherwise, merits serious consideration by all our churches and the Ulster public.' The SDLP, through Paddy O'Donoghue, the member for South Down, said that his party was in favour of integrated education, subject to the rights of parents to send their children to schools of their choice being protected in any new scheme. The Catholic Irish National Teachers' Organisation welcomed the proposals saying that it had been on record since 1969 as favouring mixed schooling. The mainly Protestant Ulster Teachers' Union said that it supported the proposals, as did the National Association of Schoolmasters.

Sinn Féin criticised me for deliberately ignoring the major source of the strife in Northern Ireland, namely the English policy over the years of divide and conquer. Its policy envisaged 'integration of the schools when there has been a British withdrawal from Ireland and, hopefully, an Ulster Parliament for nine counties'.

I was agreeably surprised to learn of support from Jack Lynch. Speaking on 6 May 1974, he said:

> If segregated education is not the main source of the difficulties facing the North it is hard to argue that it is not a contributory factor to the fears and misunderstandings now existing between the various sections of the population there.... Many young people in the North are adversely influenced towards their neighbours by the religious environments in which they were reared.

He said he hoped my proposals would receive sympathetic consideration from all church authorities.

Sadly this was not to be the case. Predictably adverse reaction came from some clergy. Canon Padraig Murphy, a prominent Catholic priest, argued vehemently on television against the proposals, declaring them to be contrary to the duty of Catholics, and saying they would 'not find favour with those who wish to uphold the principles of our religion, and the attendance of our children at Catholic schools is to do with that'. On the same programme the Reverend Donald Gillies, a Presbyterian minister, expressed reservations about the scheme. 'I would be inclined to agree with Canon Murphy here,' he said. 'I respect the position of the Roman Catholic Church in asking to bring to their children the message of the Christian faith as they see it.'

A Church of Ireland Board of Education report at the time took the view that it seemed likely that Protestants would not be ready for integration so long as the Catholic Church maintained its attitude to inter-church marriages. It was equally likely, the report said, that Catholics would not be ready for integration so long as they saw integration as a way of removing their schools from the influence of their church. So, it concluded, 'any prospects of integration can only be seen within the context of relations within the community'. The report added that the main concern of the Church of Ireland was the encouragement of harmony and good relations within the community. To that end the Church of Ireland would welcome, within the state and voluntary systems of education, agreed experiments towards encouraging integration in education on the understanding that denominational interests were respected.

The Moderator of the Presbyterian Church, Dr John Orr, said the plan would have to be carefully studied but that already in 1971 the General Assembly had passed a resolution in favour of integrated schools. He said the Presbyterian Church would be fully prepared to examine my proposals and would encourage them. I was delighted that the Reverend Harold Sloan, president of my own Methodist Church, gave a warm welcome in principle to my statement.

It was abundantly clear from some of these responses that if I was to wait for the churches to come up with their own proposals it would be a long wait. But my plan was killed in infancy with the collapse of the Executive over the following three weeks. According to John Taylor, it was the only creative idea that emanated from the powersharing Executive.

Throughout their short and turbulent tenure, members of the Executive doggedly carried out routine duties and ran their departments as if the Executive had a future. Amongst many engagements, I paid official visits to museums, distributed prizes, and addressed the annual Ulster Teachers' Union conference.

I remember the 1974 annual grammar school headmasters' conference at Ballygally, at which I was guest speaker. In the audience was the headmaster of a large grammar school who had been my Greek and Latin teacher at Methody. He had been an exacting teacher, demanding high standards, intolerant of weaknesses. One day, when we were translating the *Apologia* of Socrates, he had accused me of having copied something from my friend Niall Rudd. I had vehemently protested my innocence but was not believed, and was so stung by the injustice that I had promised myself that some day in the big world outside there would be an occasion when I would get my revenge. Here was the opportunity. The passage of time, however, had diminished and mollified, if not totally wiped out, the memory. I am glad to say we stood each other drinks and chatted together at the bar.

The opportunities to enjoy the fruits of office, to say nothing of ordinary domestic life, were rare in those few months before the fall of the Executive. I had little time to play the piano, my favourite pastime. This was evident when, in early May, Roisin Walsh came to interview me for Ulster Television at Lambeg where we were now living. In the course of the interview she asked if I would play something. I was foolhardy enough to do so, choosing a Chopin nocturne. In the next day's issue of the *Irish Times* I was described unkindly as the 'Chopin-rending' minister. I had more luck when the cameras filmed me putting on the eighth green at Malone golf course. Untypically, a putt rolled in from about fifteen feet. It was a rare stroke of luck.

Ian Paisley was persuaded that Rome was behind the powersharing experiment, and that Brian Faulkner, who had referred to Paisley as 'the demon doctor', was the ultimate heretic who had to be destroyed. The manner of Faulkner's going was suggested at the time by one political wit among his enemies:

> And there was wee Brian Faulkner, sitting on a great big chair, looking just as proud as the Pope of Rome himself – and his wee legs were wrapped round the legs of the chair, and I said to my companion, either we're going to have to saw his legs off, or the chair's legs off, to get him off that chair.

But it was the Ulster Workers' Council (UWC) strike that pulled Faulkner off the big chair, a strike not initially supported by Paisley, though he quickly jumped on the bandwagon once he saw how effectively it would roll.

The strike began on the day the Executive won the Sunningdale vote in the Assembly – Tuesday, 14 May 1974. What followed was an extraordinary rebellion by the vast majority of one million Protestants, which brought down a government with hardly a shot being fired. Northern Ireland became ungovernable, with the British authorities completely impotent. It was a cleverly organised and meticulous operation with David Trimble, then a constitutional lawyer at Queen's University and an official of Bill Craig's Vanguard Party, among those supporting the strike. The propaganda and public relations efforts of the strike committee and their later 'provisional government' were impressive.

The strike was a nightmarish, surreal experience. Gradually the power stations were run down to near the 'point of no return' when a complete shutdown would be inevitable. It was a point of honour for us to carry on fulfilling public engagements even when lights failed. This happened when I attended a violin recital: the shadow of the soloist fell sinisterly across the white walls of the Harty Room at Queen's University as he played in candlelight.

Barricades, watched over by grim-looking men in dark glasses and hooded coats, were put up in Protestant areas, and with dwindling petrol supplies it became increasingly difficult to move about. Members of the Executive, including myself, had to be transported to Stormont either by helicopter or in armed convoy.

We waited with growing anxiety for Harold Wilson's promise of military action. As no orders had been given to the army in face of what was clearly going to be an effective strike, I wondered whether the British were prepared to trust the Executive any longer. Clearly, decisions were being taken without any reference to the Executive. At home I was subjected to intimidatory phone calls: 'We know where to get you, you Fitt-lover.' Only a few phoned anxiously pleading that we 'hang on'. Bombs went off in Dublin and Monaghan killing twenty-eight people, probably the work of Protestant extremists. The Ulster Workers' Council set up a 'provisional government' and issued petrol ration passes. The army concluded it could not run Ballylumford power station without the help of senior staff, and took no action to remove UDA barricades. They and, it seemed, the British government were reluctant to break the strike by force.

By Tuesday, 21 May, only five main roads were open and shops and companies started negotiations with the Ulster Workers' Council, which began issuing instructions to the population at large. By Thursday it was clear that the strike would succeed. Appeals to Prime Minister Harold Wilson followed. He responded on Saturday, 25 May, with his disastrous nationwide television speech referring to Northern Ireland people as 'spongers'. He described the strike as a 'deliberate and calculated attempt to use every undemocratic and unparliamentary means for the purpose of bringing down the whole constitution of Northern Ireland so as to set up a sectarian and undemocratic state, from which one-third of the people would be excluded'. The organisers, he said, were 'thugs and bullies'.

> The people on this side of the water, British parents, British tax-payers, have seen their sons villified, spat upon and murdered. They have seen the taxes they have poured out almost without regard to cost – over £300 million a year this year with the cost of the Army operations on top of that – going into Northern Ireland. They see property destroyed by evil violence and are asked to pick up the bill for rebuilding it. Yet people who benefit from this now viciously defy Westminster, purporting to act as though they were an elected government, spend their lives sponging on Westminster and British democracy and then systematically assault democratic methods.

In exasperation he ended up by asking: 'Who do these people think they are?'

This ill-judged statement knocked the props from under the Executive. After this we were really rearranging the deck chairs on the *Titanic*. Next day thousands of tiny sponges appeared pinned to the lapels of the loyalists' jackets. A total strike was called for Monday, the 27th, and immediately there was the threat of widespread sewerage floods and river and water supply pollution.

A desperate attempt was made by the Unionists in the Executive to agree to a phasing-in of the Council of Ireland, that is, to abandon setting up a full Council of Ireland with executive powers and two parliamentary tiers until the next election for the Northern Ireland

Assembly in 1977–78. The SDLP met in another room to consider our
suggestions on how we could be unhooked from the Council of
Ireland proposal, something that Paddy Devlin and Gerry Fitt tried
unsuccessfully to achieve. As can be imagined, morale around the
Executive table was at an all-time low as the SDLP met their back-
benchers in an attempt to secure some sort of renegotiation. Nor was
it likely to improve with Roy Bradford breaking ranks when, without consultation, he urged talks with the Ulster Workers' Council,
whose headquarters he had openly visited ten days before. There was
a blazing row in the Executive about his breach of the principles of
collective responsibility which the Executive had from the beginning
agreed to operate; most of us would have supported the SDLP when
they demanded he be sacked. Bradford did offer his resignation, but
Brian Faulkner refused to accept it as to do so would have provided
him with 'an easy way out of a tight corner and further comfort for
the UWC'.

For me the strain of the last hours of the Executive became almost
unbearable. For the first time, I experienced real, stomach-gripping
fear. Our efforts at putting together and keeping in position a coalition
government were soon to be proved a total waste of time and physical
and emotional effort. The last chance had gone, and I did not believe
there would be another in my lifetime. I could appreciate the cynicism
of the Chinese curse: 'May you live in exciting times.'

Close to tears, I went next door into an empty committee room
quietly to address the Almighty on the crisis, and to ask was there not
something He could do about it? But I remembered the cautionary
story of the Ohio farmer and his son as a tornado spiralled its way
towards them. When the boy dropped to his knees to pray for deliver-
ance his father shouted: 'Run like hell, son, scared prayers ain't worth a
damn.' I rejoined my colleagues without any lively hope that the SDLP
could go along with our suggestion to put the Council of Ireland on the
long finger.

It had been an extraordinary fourteen days. Was all this indicative of
a fundamental Ulster nationalism, or of a working-class radicalism?
The immediate consequences were clear enough, with hundreds of

thousands of jubilant loyalists taking to the Belfast streets to rejoice in the fall of the Executive. And God's hand in the fate of the Executive was acknowledged by the singing of 'Oh God our help in ages past' in the UWC headquarters by the workers and politicians, as with satisfaction they contemplated their handiwork. Meanwhile, effigies of Faulkner and Fitt were burnt in the streets. It was a sobering thought that the Executive had a larger minority against it when it fell than did the old Stormont government in the last moments of its power two years earlier.

Many would argue that the strike was out of all proportion to the threat posed to Northern Ireland's existence by the reforms being implemented by the liberal Unionists and the SDLP. Liberal Unionists especially were the targets for loyalist bitterness and anger. With hindsight, and though lessons would of course be learned, the strike put back considerably the prospects for a political resolution to Northern Ireland's fundamental problems. Subsequent events only increased polarisation.

Nevertheless, the Executive was not brought down by the strikers alone. The majority of Protestants simply did not want the Executive and were passive supporters of the strike. Glenn Barr, a moving spirit, said later that he was surprised at the ease with which the Executive had fallen. It was of little consolation to me years later when several of those centrally involved in its fall admitted to me that they had been mistaken. One key player said he wished he had been with us!

If the Executive had not fallen and we had been given support for the four years that Harold Wilson had promised, it is just possible that, working together in the interests of all the people of Northern Ireland, the Executive could have put in place some of the elements of the current peace process twenty years earlier. However, in 1974 there was not enough trust between the two communities to make the Executive, never mind Sunningdale, work.

The week after the strike, dejected, I made my way back to the Bar Library at the Royal Courts of Justice. In the large hall I met a very senior member of the Supreme Court Bench who said to me as he made his way briskly towards the main exit, 'Maybe now the Brits will allow us to do our own thing.' I realised then the extent to which the strike had received the imprimatur of the establishment as well as of the middle and working classes that placed the demands of our Ulster heritage above those of British rule and who, as Maurice Hayes put it, 'transferred their allegiance to the organisers of the strike once they saw where their personal advantage lay'. I remained convinced, however, that a powersharing formula of some description was the only way forward for Northern Ireland.

On a more personal level, I knew that in attempting to roll the stone back up the hill again at the Bar I could not expect to have many friends amongst those who provided the work. Moreover, many of those junior to me had streaked away out of sight. My seniority was gone. Brian Faulkner came to see me at Lambeg to thank me for my support during those trying years and to say how sorry he was at the way things had worked out. 'Twice,' he said, 'you have followed me into the wilderness.'

Early in 1977 I wrote to congratulate him on his life peerage. In his reply he said that although powersharing had cost him his political career, at least we had laid an educational foundation stone, if nothing else. I came to like and admire him as a man whose buoyancy, optimism and capacity to face the most difficult challenges did much for my morale. His brisk, reassuring manner was one aspect of his leadership qualities which were such that I would have followed him almost anywhere – and did. I shall remember especially his diplomatic skill in terminating lengthy and difficult cabinet discussions and his adroitness in reviewing differing opinions, picking up the argument at the point of balance. Every minister felt that his views had been given due weight and consideration. I remember Faulkner with much affection, and it was a sad personal loss when in March 1977 he met his death in a riding accident. This happened not far away from where I am writing this book, at my present home at the Spa, County Down. The cottage has a view of the Mourne Mountains, and as I write, I can see across the valley to his last resting place, at Magherahamlet Presbyterian church, on the side of a distant drumlin.

After the fall of the Executive, Faulkner had been keen for me to continue in politics with the new moderate Unionist Party of Northern Ireland which he was to launch in September 1974, but I had had enough and preferred to leave the field of play to those who could better please the 'madding crowd'. Furthermore, family responsibilities had to take priority now. I could afford to take no more risks.

In September 1974, Martin McBirney QC, a resident magistrate, was assassinated by the IRA at his home in Belmont, Belfast. I was invited to replace him. I refused at first, prepared to tough it out at the Bar. However, a reasonable pay cheque at the end of the month and pension provision were things I had never had. They were too attractive to reject, despite the security risk. But, strangely, it was with no great joy that I quit the stormy waters of politics and the Bar and decided to put in to port.

8

RELATIVE CALM

MY WORKING LIFE HENCEFORTH was dramatically trans-
formed. From now on, I would have a captive audience,
obliged to get to its feet every morning as I entered court
to the cry of 'Silence in court – all stand!' I now took on the resident
magistrate's role and mantle of omniscience. That judges have an
instinctive knowledge of the skills necessary for their job has until
recently been assumed without question. This assumption has no basis
whatsoever. Happily today judicial training, through the Judicial
Studies Board, is regarded by the judiciary not merely as a duty, but a
right.

Sitting on the Bench presented a vastly different experience from
politics. Never again would I be assailed by shouts of 'rubbish!

nonsense! traitor!' Instead I would be listened to attentively and (mostly) with respect. I had the last word in my own court. Anyone dissatisfied with my decisions could appeal to a higher court. That was the theory.

One morning, however, when presiding in the drab and dreary Number 2 Court in Belfast (the Custody Court) I had a problem when a ruling I made in the case before me was angrily questioned. The difficulty arose when a defendant refused to speak in English but chose to speak in Irish. Proceedings in Northern Ireland courts, as in England, are ordinarily conducted in English. The rule is that when a foreigner who has no English is on trial, and is undefended, the evidence given must be translated to him. On this occasion the accused was unrepresented but he was from west Belfast and I was not prepared to accept that he could be regarded as a foreigner. When the charge was put to him he responded in Irish. When I asked him to repeat what he had said and he responded again in Irish, I thought it not unreasonable to assume that he could understand English. This was confirmed when a police officer testified on oath that down in the cells, before the accused was brought up, he was heard to ask a friend, 'What have they got *you* for?' During the bilingual exchanges in court a large, bearded man in the body of the court rose to his feet and offered to translate, saying he was a fluent Irish speaker. I advised him that it was for the court to appoint an interpreter who would be asked to swear by Almighty God that he would 'well and faithfully interpret, and explanation make of, all such matters and things as should be required of him according to the best of his skill and understanding'. As I did not know him, his reliability would have to be investigated and this could not be done there and then. I rejected his offer, upon which he proceeded to remonstrate and was quickly removed from the court. When he had left, another member of the public, a dark-haired young man with his coat over his arm, as if about to leave the court, complained that he had never witnessed such injustice. He insisted the accused was entitled to speak in Irish and that if this was the type of justice this court was dispensing then it could only do harm to the public's confidence in the judicial system. I could not let this pass, and ordered that he be arrested for contempt of court, advising him that I would retire for ten minutes to enable him to review his position and, I hoped, decide to purge his contempt by offering an apology.

What amounts to contempt of court is not altogether clear. Certainly to throw something at the Bench would be. But it was at least arguable that his haranguing the Bench was not, and that the issue as to whether it was or was not could have been the subject of a separate hearing. Back in my room I fervently hoped that he would apologise. He did – and very handsomely. He ought to have known better, he said, and by the time he was through with his generous apology I had begun to reproach myself at having in the first place taken such a high-handed course. But he had, I reminded myself, challenged the Bench before a court packed to capacity, and I had felt it necessary to uphold the dignity of the court.

I suspected that this was an attempt to have a case conducted in Irish for political purposes. Sadly, the Irish language has become associated for Protestants with the cult of murderous violence, whilst by nationalists its restoration and use is often presented as one of the best hopes of a united Ireland. The task of dissociating Irish-language culture from militant republicanism has in recent years been taken in hand by the Northern Ireland Community Relations Council through the establishment in 1990 of the Ultach Trust, which has the twin aims of widening appreciation of the contribution made by the Irish language to the culture of Northern Ireland and of increasing knowledge of the language through all sections of the community. Today it is good to see the encouragement of the Irish language in schools and the new interest in it shown by many Protestants who attend Irish-language extramural classes at Queen's University and elsewhere.

My life on the Bench has had its problems. Over the past three decades of civil strife, the pressures on judges, resident magistrates and court officials have inevitably been enormous. In difficult and dangerous circumstances the courts have continued to operate and uphold the rule of law with courage and dignity. Three judges and two magistrates have been assassinated by the IRA, two others have been seriously injured, and most of us have received threats. On three occasions members of the RUC Special Branch have come to my home to warn me to be careful as, according to 'good-grade' information, I was on an IRA 'list'. My personal safety meant many restaurants and golf clubs, for example, being put out of bounds. My freedom of movement generally has been seriously curtailed.

Undermining the court system has always been a priority for the revolutionary terrorist. Court staff have suffered their share of intimidation and danger when court buildings have been targeted. Despite the risk of being 'part of the British war machine' (the terrorist reason for threatening life and destroying court property) the courts have continued to operate normally, and the people of Northern Ireland will recognise the debt they owe to a courts system that has stood between them and anarchy.

The jurisdiction of the magistrate's court is diverse. It is here that members of the general public are most likely to see the law in operation as these courts hear over 90 per cent of all cases that come before the courts. 'All life is there', and with sometimes well over one hundred cases listed in a day, the heat and burden of it all requires the exercise of a great deal of composure by the presiding magistrate.

During the 1980s I sat in the Custody Court in Belfast at a time when rioting in the city was at its height. These cases normally involved a complete conflict of evidence, down to inches when it came to who was standing where at the critical time. When it comes to one witness's word against another's, the truth is hard to discover. Truth does not present itself to all alike, and there is always the problem of the truth being told badly and a lie well. In the end, where there is no independent evidence to assist the court, it is left to decide subjectively where it believes the truth lies, taking into account the demeanour of witnesses in the witness box. Even then, 'there's no art to find the mind's construction in the face'.

Sometimes riot cases assumed the importance of state trials, with standing room only in the court. Those living in the area where the riot occurred were there to provide moral support for their youngsters. Resentment against the police and army was often palpable, and defence lawyers were well aware of the value of this for publicity purposes. They would accordingly embark on repetitive and hectoring cross-examination, often calculated to provoke the Bench. Some barristers and solicitors obviously felt that the best way to serve their client was to provoke the magistrate into an impatient reaction leading to an unedifying exchange and the subsequent complaint that their client was obviously not likely to have a fair hearing as the magistrate was hostile and had already made up his mind. It is the stock in trade of the combative lawyer to try to force witnesses into discrepancies on thoroughly insignificant detail and to waste an enormous amount of time rehashing each tiny fact. The lawyer who keeps the fighting well away from the main issue by manufacturing tiny subplots hopes to divert attention away from the obvious guilt of the client. Attempting to get some of them to move on was seldom successful. I learned that it was better to avoid descending into the arena and making matters worse – precisely the object of wild cross-examination.

Between 1981 and 1986 the supergrass system was used to produce informers willing to give evidence in court against alleged fellow terrorists. It was strongly defended by the British government and the RUC as being well established in English law. Informers came from the Provisional IRA (including Christoper Black and Raymond Gilmour), the Irish National Liberation Army (including Harry Kirkpatrick and Jackie Grimley), and the UVF, of whom 'Budgie' Allen was one of the best-known members. In the period 1981 to 1983, evidence from nearly thirty supergrasses led to charges against some three hundred people. Thirteen of the supergrasses ultimately retracted their evidence before their trials began. Others were given immunity from prosecution, police protection, and the means to start a new life outside Northern Ireland. I was asked would I take the Budgie Allen preliminary investigation, due to start on 15 August 1984, which would involve the calling of Crown witnesses to ascertain whether there was a prima-facie case against the accused.

Budgie Allen, also known as William Reeves after his stepfather, grew up in the fiercely loyalist Shankill area of Belfast. He acquired the nickname 'Budgie' at primary school, in reference to the character played by Adam Faith in the television programme of that name. Ironically, it was later to assume fresh significance when he was prepared to repeat whatever was suggested to him against his colleagues in the UVF when police were interviewing him. Like a budgie, it was said, Allen was willing and able to repeat whatever he had been told.

On 9 April 1984 Allen had pleaded guilty to fifty-two offences arising out of twenty-six incidents, including attempted murder, conspiracy to murder, possession of firearms and explosives, giving and receiving training in the use of firearms and explosives, robbery, and membership of the UVF. He was sentenced to a total of fourteen years on all charges.

Before I entered Number 1 Court at Crumlin Road courthouse on the morning of 15 August to begin a preliminary investigation on a number of alleged loyalist paramilitaries, I was told that their lawyers were saying that the inquiry would not go the distance so volatile was the situation in the courtroom. I took this as a personal challenge. When I took my seat on the Bench the scene was indeed intimidating. Police officers were there in force, lining the area occupied by a number of the accused who had been remanded in custody and would be produced for identification by Budgie Allen. On my left in the jury box were those of the accused on bail. I looked up to see the gallery packed with relations and supporters of the accused men. Amongst those in the gallery was George Seawright, a militant loyalist politician from the Shankill area of Belfast who had been elected to Belfast City Council in 1981 and to the Assembly of 1982 on the slogan 'A Protestant candidate for a Protestant people'. (He had recently been expelled from the Democratic Unionist Party for failing to 'clarify a comment at a Belfast Education and Library Board meeting that "Catholics and their priests should be burned"', following objections by Catholic parents to the playing of the British national anthem at joint school concerts – an incident which also led to a three-month suspended sentence and a £100 fine.) He was a regular visitor to the preliminary inquiry and his personal protection weapon was removed by the police at the door of the courthouse each morning. The inquiry promised to be an interesting experience.

Allen went into the dock and was duly sworn to tell the truth, the whole truth and nothing but the truth. But we had scarcely got going when a solicitor for one of the accused interrupted Crown counsel to ask if his client could be excused to go to the toilet. It was 11.30 a.m. I discreetly asked whether any of the others were in the same plight, and discovered that a number of them were. It was not unreasonable to assume that this was a ploy to interrupt the proceedings while the police escorted their charges from the courtroom and back again. I expressed the hope that they would all manage until 1.00 p.m. when the court would rise for lunch.

The next interruption was when one of the accused dismissed his counsel and became disruptive. I had power to hear the case against the accused in his absence in those circumstances, and I had him removed to the cells below where, I told him, he would have the advantage of hearing the proceedings on the intercom system with which the cells were equipped. Shortly after this, word came up to me from a solicitor that his client could not hear the proceedings. I discovered that this was because he had pulled the wires out of the loudspeakers.

An essential part of Budgie Allen's evidence was the identification of those in court he was 'fingering' as alleged members of the UVF and with whom he had allegedly been at meetings and drilling exercises around Ballymena. Unfortunately this identification procedure necessitated him, in some cases, leaving the witness box to go over to where the accused he was trying to identify had 'ducked' down below the back of the seat in front and could not be seen.

Frequent interruptions, general restlessness and shouts from the gallery made the orderly conduct of the proceedings extremely difficult during the first week. During the second week, towards the end of the proceedings, I noticed that one of the accused, Frenchie Marchant, had removed his glasses which he had been wearing up to then. I became suspicious that something unpleasant might be afoot and at lunchtime suggested this to the inspector in charge of the RUC contingent. He did not share my fears, and even if he had there was little he could have done to prevent what eventually happened.

Shortly after resuming that afternoon and just as Allen was signing his lengthy deposition against one of the accused, a woman in the public gallery, said to have been his mother, shouted, 'Don't sign, Budgie!' and hurled a packet of birdseed down towards him. Other missiles swiftly followed and a pitched battle erupted in which four police officers were slightly injured and four members of the public were arrested. Before adjourning the proceedings and leaving the Bench, I warned those on my left who were on bail that if they joined in the disturbance their bail was in jeopardy. I retired to my room with, I hope, as much dignity as I could muster in the circumstances. On resumption of the proceedings I excluded the public from the remainder of the hearings.

I returned for trial all fifty-six of those accused on 227 charges on Allen's evidence, half being released on bail and half remanded in custody. Some of those accused had dismissed their lawyers, claiming they had no expectation of a fair hearing. They and others of the defendants were later acquitted on the grounds that the evidence of a supergrass was suspect and not satisfactory, and could not produce sustainable convictions. Nevertheless, the evidence given by super-grasses had provided the police with information as to the *modus operandi* of terrorist organisations.

Another unpleasant preliminary inquiry over which I presided con-cerned the murders in March 1988 of army corporals Derek Wood and David Howes of the Signals Regiment who were caught up in the funeral procession of IRA man Kevin Brady who had been killed three days earlier by the loyalist Michael Stone. This too was held in Court Number 1 at Crumlin Road courthouse, set up for the hearing with television monitors and attended by the international press crammed into the jury box.

The unfortunate soldiers, dressed in civilian clothes (they had arrived in Northern Ireland the previous week), had for some reason or other been in the area of Milltown cemetery driving in the direc-tion of the funeral cortege, when their car was blocked from behind by a black taxi. The windows of the car were smashed and the two were dragged out. One soldier fired a warning shot before they were overpowered.

Overhead, an army surveillance helicopter crew filmed in terrible detail the last moments of the soldiers' lives. The evidence against the three accused before me in the dock was mainly provided by film from which the Crown alleged they could be identified as three of those involved in the murders. I shall not forget the horror of what was shown on the screens. The hapless young men, who had been brutally manhandled in the taxi taking them to their place of execution, were seen stripped to their underpants, fighting bravely to the last before being shot several times while they lay on the ground.

I returned two of the accused for trial. In respect of the third, who was alleged to have been directing the taxi at the point where the young men were killed, being unable to see any evidence of identification upon which a court could connect him with the murders, I discharged him.

I have often wondered why, when it was seen from the helicopter what was happening, the crew did not call up help, or alternatively descend to a height at which the turbulence created by the propellers might have saved the soldiers. The short answer probably was that to get involved in that way would risk the helicopter being exposed to ground fire. The truth seems to be that the soldiers were left to their fate on instructions from the authorities with whom the helicopter would have been in contact, because they could not be saved without further loss of life.

On 1 June 1989 two men from Andersonstown in west Belfast were sentenced to life imprisonment for these murders at the first of a number of trials connected with the killings. Later, I was often to be reminded of those barbaric scenes, for painted for all to see on a remote and narrow country road near where we live in County Down, at a point about halfway along a favourite six-mile walk, there was the message:

REMEMBER
DEREK WOOD AND DAVID HOWES
MARCH 1988

Not until recently was this obviously threatening command obliterated when the road was resurfaced. I for one shall not forget.

I retired from being a full-time resident magistrate in June 1993, since when I have been acting as a deputy. My appointment as a resident magistrate allowed me the time and freedom to indulge other interests, mainly in education. Shortly after the fall of the powersharing Executive in 1974 I was invited to join the board of governors of Campbell College where we had sent our two sons; I was subsequently a governor for sixteen years. What has given me most satisfaction and fulfilment, however, has been my involvement in the foundation in 1981 of Lagan College, the first deliberately planned integrated secondary school in Northern Ireland.

9

BREAKING THE MOULD

HAD IT NOT BEEN FOR MY ROLE in the powersharing Executive, I very much doubt whether I would have taken up the cause of integrated education. Prior to entering politics, my middle-class, sheltered and comfortable background concealed from me the effect a segregated system of education had in perpetuating and reinforcing the deep divide in Northern Ireland society. I had never been implicated in the region's social apartheid. My schooldays in Fermanagh brought me into daily contact with Catholic boys and girls who seemed in no way different from myself. It is a self-evident truth that it is a matter of considerable difficulty to prevent youngsters from associating with those of a different colour, race, creed or rank, because, left to themselves, children disregard all such distinctions. An easy association with Catholics followed me through to Queen's University where many of my friends came from the Catholic community.

The adverse social and political effects of segregated education were soon to dawn upon me. I came to realise that children separately educated in Catholic and Protestant schools absorbed in their own homes a series of attitudes, had them confirmed amongst their peers and were, to a great extent, shaped and moulded for their adult lives. Education, in the sense of providing academic wallpaper, was doing the task for which it was traditionally responsible, but was unable or unfitted to go further.

I had official contact with the mindset produced by segregation at the time I was minister of education; one of these encounters involved two schools in Belfast within yards of each other, but governed under differing religious systems. At the end of the day, the pupils were released within minutes of each other, and every day police had to be deployed to ensure that street conflict was prevented. The schools were from a different cultural background, and each to the other was the enemy. The separateness of the pupil's backgrounds, the narrowness of their social, as distinct from formal, education, the importance of beliefs and traditions so cramped and limited their thinking as to create a background of hostility that could only find expression in hatred and violence which they would probably carry into adult life.

The suffering of Northern Ireland children, particularly during the violent unrest of the 1970s, was movingly illustrated in the simplest language – the language of children – in a note from a boy in a Belfast secondary school that was published in the *Northern Teacher*.

My daddy is dead 4 weeks now, and that's a month. He died on a Wednesday morning at half past six. He was beaten up in August because he tried to stop them burning the houses in our street. He was in hospital 4 weeks before he died. My daddy said to me when he was living, he said when you grow up you will be a man like me. He said that because I bring dogs and cats into the house and so did he. He brought home fish and all. My mammy said he died happy because he died in his sleep. When the smoke

started coming from the walls of our house we ran out and down
the entry. My budgy and frogs and my cat and a hamster were
burned in the house. This was the second time we were burned
out. When the slates were cracking with the heat we thought it
was guns and we cut over into another entry and went to our
granny's house. My aunt gave me a dog. I call it Arkle. I have a
wishing well and I save up money in it. When I have three
shillings I will buy a goldfish.

I came across another deeply moving example of the suffering of a
child. When the Troubles in Belfast were at their height, many gave
their time to visit riot areas. One visitor found a woman in tears in her
home in a street that was half burned out. The explanation for her tears
was not the destruction, but a letter she had found in her eight-year-old
daughter's pocket. The letter was addressed to the child's friend who
had lived in one of the houses now burned. It read:

Some men I did not know came and set your furniture in the
street. They broke it up but they did not touch your pram and
they did not touch your dollies. They burned your house and
broke your windows. I do not understand any of this. I hope I
shall be able to play with you again.

There is an awesome simplicity and openness about these two notes that
chilled me when I first read them, and still does. One child was a Catholic, the other a Protestant.

Arguments against segregated education in Ireland were recognised
over 150 years ago but, as Professor John Darby of the University of
Ulster reminds us, the occasional pioneering experiments designed to
alter the existing educational practice have regularly been accompanied
by crises:

... how frequently the crises have been the result of the same dispute – the extent to which the Churches should control the
schools. ... the central dispute was never about religion but
about power, and may at one time have had some historical
justification. Religion was the identifying mark of division, but
not its essence.

In 1826, three years before the enactment of Catholic Emancipation, Dr Doyle, Catholic Bishop of Kildare and Leighlin, whom Thackeray (in his *Irish Sketch Book* of 1843) described as 'the best champion the Catholic Church and cause ever had in Ireland', said:

> I do not know of any measures which would prepare the way for a better feeling in Ireland, than uniting the children at an early age and bringing them up in the same school leading them to commune with one another and to form those little intimacies and friendships which often subsist through life.

And giving evidence before a parliamentary committee, he said:

> I do not see how any man wishing well to the public peace and who looks to Ireland as his country, can think that peace can be permanently established, or the prosperity of the country ever well secured, if children are separated at the commencement of life on account of their religious beliefs.

The harmonious spirit in which the Catholic Church engineered the setting up of the system of 'national schools' in Ireland in the 1830s, regarded by the Presbyterians as something of a victory for Catholics (so much so that the clergy of the two Protestant churches refused to join the system for a time), comes as something of a surprise to us today.

Lord Londonderry, the first minister of education for Northern Ireland one hundred years later, disliked segregated education, recognising it as one of the principal ways in which divisions in the community were perpetuated; he believed that a system of integrated schools would best secure the stability of the young state. Separate schooling, he believed, would endanger the public peace in the aftermath of the partition of Ireland.

So, the integrated schools issue is not new – it has been a staple of education debate in Ireland for more than one and a half centuries. In the 1960s the debate became even more lively as a result of the onset of community violence, with some Catholic clergy voicing approval of the idea of shared-site schools and common facilities at sixth-form level. In 1971 the Presbyterian General Assembly passed a resolution declaring that 'integrated education would best serve the social, economic and educational needs of the community'. It was public pressure, however, that led to change.

In the 1970s a group of Catholic parents in the north Down and east Belfast area came together to provide catechism classes for their children who were attending non-Catholic schools. The Catholic Church in Northern Ireland does not have Sunday schools, nor does it wish to instruct Catholic children in non-Catholic schools. In some cases the sacrament of Confirmation was even withheld from children attending non-Catholic schools. These parents founded the All Children Together (ACT) movement, the aim of which was to seek changes in the education system of Northern Ireland that would make it possible for parents who so wished to secure for their children an education in shared schools acceptable to all religious denominations and cultures and in which the churches would provide religious education and also, importantly, pastoral care. In 1974, the original Catholic parents were joined by Protestant parents who wished to work with them to press church and state to develop integrated schools within existing school structures.

At that time I was putting forward my 'shared schools' initiative to the Assembly. Preoccupied with getting this plan on to the agenda, I was only vaguely aware of the existence of the All Children Together movement. I did not know, nor was I in touch with, any of its members. We were heading down the same road but had not as yet caught up with each other.

When my 'shared schools' plan fell with the Executive, I decided not to abandon the issue. The new British administration made it clear that it did not intend to proceed with my plans, the minister responsible at the time for education, Lord Melchett, stating that there was a lack of 'a substantial agreement in favour of the idea'. There were, however, I knew, concerned parents working away with the same aims and objects in mind, who might be interested in taking me with them. And so I asked Cecilia Linehan, an orthodontist from Holywood, County Down, who had stood as an Alliance candidate in the Assembly elections, and Tony Spencer, a lecturer in the Faculty of Sociology at Queen's University, founders of ACT, if I could be of any help. They welcomed me on board.

The aims and objects of ACT were formally adopted at the inaugural general meeting of the association on 28 January 1977:

> The All Children Together Movement seeks change in the education system in Northern Ireland, that will make it possible for parents who so wish, to secure for their children an education in Shared Schools acceptable to all religious denominations and cultures, in which the Churches will provide religious education and pastoral care.

Peter Melchett's response was that although no bill would be introduced in support of shared schools, future legislative changes, including the reorganisation of secondary schooling, 'should not create or perpetuate barriers against integrated schooling'. This was not of any great assistance to our idea of integrated education, more in line with Clough's 'Thou shalt not kill; but need'st not strive / Officiously to keep alive'.

We started thinking about how the law could be changed to facilitate and protect integration. After discussions between ACT and Protestant educational spokesmen in 1977, Tony Spencer produced a draft private Bill which aimed to create a third sector in the educational system, an integrated sector, to exist alongside the maintained (Catholic) and the controlled (*de facto* Protestant) sectors. The suggested legislation would also allow the 'transferors' (the representatives of the Protestant churches in state schools) and the 'trustees' (the representatives of the Catholic Church in maintained schools) to give any school a new-style integrated committee: one-third parents' representatives, one-third Area Board members and one-third Church representatives – equally divided between the Catholic and the Protestant churches.

As I had suggested previously to the Assembly, it was important to have the support and goodwill of the churches. A second objective in the strategy was to persuade the churches' representatives in suitable cases to take the initiative.

Previously at their synods, conferences and assemblies Protestant churches had affirmed their desire for integration. Moreover, the Catholic hierarchy had stressed the importance and the right of parental choice in matters of education. The Catholic Church had, after all, adapted itself to shared educational schemes in England, Kenya, Tanzania, and indeed parts of Northern Ireland.

As Northern Ireland no longer had a legislature and as this would be a private Bill, the only way of getting it onto the statute book was through the House of Lords. Only government measures affecting Northern Ireland could be introduced into law in the House of Commons by Orders in Council – and integrated education in Northern Ireland was not likely to be on the government's political agenda.

I took the draft Bill to Fred Martin, the Parliamentary Draftsman at Stormont, who very kindly and courageously (for this was not a government measure) got his staff to knock it into shape. This was done so expertly that the draftsmen in the House of Lords could find no fault in the drafting. At the same time I wrote to Brian Faulkner (by now Lord Faulkner) asking if he would agree to pilot the Bill through the House of Lords. Sadly, my letter arrived at Highlands on the day he was tragically killed by a fall from his horse. Lord Dunleath, who had been an Alliance Party member of the Assembly, agreed to take it up.

The Second Reading of the Bill, entitled 'An Act to facilitate the establishment in Northern Ireland of schools to be attended by pupils of different religious affiliations or cultural traditions', came before the House of Lords on 23 June 1977. At 10 a.m. that morning I went to see the Methodist guru of Speakers' Corner and Tower Hill fame, Lord Soper, the superintendent minister of the West London Methodist Mission. When I entered his office at Kingsway Hall Methodist Church, the great man was gloomily sitting with his feet up on his desk. He had to officiate at the funeral of the son of a close friend that afternoon, and was doubtful when I asked whether he would be able to get down to the House of Lords to take part in the debate. Besides, he did not get much pleasure out of speaking in the Lords which, he told me, he avoided as much as possible. Nevertheless, he would make every effort to do so, and would I brief him on the issues raised in the Bill? I waited in the gallery of the House of Lords listening to the speeches, hoping against hope he would appear. He turned up and made his contribution to the debate later in the evening. The principle of an integrated education system was, he believed, 'inseparable from the possibility of the rising generation improving on the failures of its fathers and mothers and being able to discriminate between that which is ecclesiastically unimportant and that which is morally imperative'.

Peter Melchett, who had introduced the Second Reading without any great enthusiasm, I noted, assured the House of Lords that the government fully supported the general objectives that the Bill sought to achieve. In the end he gave it a fair wind. Others, including Terence O'Neill, warmly welcomed the measure, recognising it as an enabling step towards the inevitably slow beginning of integrated schooling. That the Catholic Archbishop of Westminster, Cardinal Hume, had already, in the course of an interview on the media with Ludovic Kennedy, given his support to integrated education was encouraging. Later, however, he was to decline my invitation to join the list of Lagan College patrons as he knew this would upset the Catholic hierarchy in Ireland.

Henry Dunleath successfully shepherded the Bill through the House of Lords, and it became at length the Education Act (NI) 1978. It owed much to his skill and dedication, but to no avail. The 1978 Act was not taken up.

Frustration with the churches and the establishment subsequently led a group of parents to take the initiative, and on 23 March 1981 they established a charitable trust to set up an integrated all-ability post-primary school in south Belfast; I was appointed chairman of the trust. The result was Lagan College, which opened its doors in September 1981 to twenty-eight pupils, two full-time teachers, two temporary teachers and a secretary (Anne Hegarty, who is still school secretary) in makeshift facilities at the Scout Activity Centre generously and coura-geously made available by the Scout authorities in the grounds of Ardnavalley (the US consul's residence).

There were two classrooms divided by a curtain through which pro-ceedings in each classroom were audible to the other. A kiosk one hundred yards away, on the main road, provided the only telephone. That enemies were lying in wait became evident when a member of the Castlereagh Urban District Council objected to the site, complain-ing that the access to and from the main road was a potential danger for the children.

When Sheila Greenfield (who had been head of the English department at Bloomfield Girls' School) accepted the post of principal she was made aware that we had no money to pay her salary. Tony and Rosemary Spencer at one stage offered to find the money by re-mortgaging their house. Sheila took the risk. Her resolution and conspicuous determination for Lagan College to succeed, which were shared by her highly principled staff of four (one of whom was a recent principal of the college, Dr Brian Lambkin, who resigned as from 1 January 1998 to take up a post as director of the Northern Ireland Centre for Emigration Studies at the Ulster American Folk Park in Omagh), were to ensure the school's survival in its profoundly difficult first years.

As an independent school, Lagan College had to demonstrate its viability over three annual intakes before seeking admission to the grant-aided system. Teachers, furniture and equipment had somehow to be procured. In the end it cost Lagan College well over half a million pounds before it was taken into the grant-aided system, and that only after the most intensive lobbying of politicians and influential figures at Westminster. Later, Secretary of State Jim Prior acknowledged to me that the pressure on him from many quarters to grant the school maintained status had become difficult to resist.

But the real credit for Lagan College must go to the parents who, in the early days, were prepared to accept the difficulties, disadvantages and risks for their children in a totally new and untried experimental initiative in education. Both parents and children were to face strong criticism and opposition. But they did this and more. Acting as fund-raisers, dinner supervisors, drivers or cleaners, they were responsible for keeping the school going at all. They persevered at considerable cost to themselves.

One working-class Catholic mother had been anxious and hesitant over choosing a secondary school for her son. When Lagan College was given publicity, an unprejudiced Catholic primary-school head teacher gave her the college brochure saying that it might provide the answer. She then took a job in a factory kitchen to earn a contribution to her son's education at the college. 'We decided,' she said, 'that no matter what happened, Christopher was going to that school. . . . My son should meet people from all walks of life.' Another parent, in sympathy with the aims of Lagan College, came from a Presbyterian background. Like others she was not herself a practising Christian, yet she found Lagan College's open-door policy to uncommitted parents a relief in the sectarian divide of our education system.

A brave couple with four children had a particular reason to support the school. As a policeman the Catholic father lived in constant danger. He sent his son to Lagan College partly because he wanted a coeducational mixed-ability school, but primarily as the only way to escape from what he saw as the overwhelming republican influence of teachers, priests and peer groups in Catholic schools. He expressed the view that the Catholic hierarchy did nothing to support those priests who pressed for a more balanced line, and he regarded Bishop Daly's refusal to appoint a Catholic priest in good standing for the doctrinal needs of the Catholic children in the school as unfortunate. One Catholic mother of two moved from the Falls Road because of the constant trouble there to the town of Antrim and sold her car to enable her to contribute towards fees and expenses. Some of the original parents took out mortgages to help maintain the school.

Nor were the children themselves less courageous. During the first year of the school, apprehensive about the reactions of their communities to their attending, they took to wearing unmarked black blazers. By the autumn of 1984 we had designed a distinctive badge for the school blazer and a school scarf: black with bright red and yellow stripes. Initially the badge was secured to the blazer with Velcro so that it could be removed before the children arrived home from school. The boys and girls now wear their uniform with real and justifiable pride.

Early in 1983 I paid a visit to Bishop Cahal Daly (now Cardinal Daly) to ask if he would send a priest in good standing to Lagan College to be responsible for the pastoral care and spiritual needs of the Catholic pupils there. The bishop received me warmly and over tea and biscuits listened intently, head deferentially to one side, to my exposition on great ecumenists of the past. I reminded him of John Wesley's letter to a Catholic written from Dublin in 1749 (edited by Michael Hurley sj) declaring what Protestant and Catholic beliefs and practice had in common, and of Bishop Doyle and his belief that peace in Ireland would be better achieved if Catholic and Protestant children were educated together under the same roof. Then, looking over to a side table on which stood a photograph of Pope John XXIII, I quoted the article of Vatican Two – *gravissima educationis* – that stated that Catholic children in schools other than Catholic schools were the responsibility of the Church.

Yes, the bishop knew all about this and he provided me with the additional information that Bishop Doyle was known as the father of Irish ecumenics. I made no impression and left with the assurance that the bishop's door was always open, and that was that.

The official position of the Catholic Church towards Lagan College and other integrated schools has to this day remained consistent since Cahal Daly became bishop of Down and Connor in 1987: the Church will do nothing to penalise Catholic parents who wish to send their children to such schools or Catholic teachers who wish to work in them. At the same time, however, the Catholic Church will do nothing that could be construed as giving official support to these schools.

That policy notwithstanding, a succession of Catholic priests and nuns have contributed to the growth of the shared chaplaincy in the college as part-time and latterly as full-time chaplains. One such was the bright, cheerful young Father Bernard Henry of the Passionists, who was popular with everybody in the school. The church authorities refused to allow him a second year with us, employing arguments of Byzantine complexity to block his reappointment. The Catholic chaplains' experiences of varying degrees of official discouragement has, perhaps understandably, been in contrast to that of the Protestant chaplains – Presbyterian, Church of Ireland, Methodist, Baptist and Non-Subscribing Presbyterian – in relation to their own church authorities.

In 1987, when Dr (later Sir) Brian Mawhinney was the Northern Ireland Office minister responsible for education, integrated education took a historic leap forward. On Tuesday, 24 March, he invited me to meet him privately at Stormont Castle. He wished to discuss a 'twin-track' initiative he had in mind towards a new government community relations policy. One of the tracks was to step up in-service teachers' training commitment on Mutual Understanding – that is, community relations education – by committing resources in a serious way to that end. The other was the creation of a trust, with endowments of £1 million in the first instance, to fund initiatives in community relations, such as community holidays, the Corrymeela Community in north Antrim, local community groups and integrated education. It was appropriate that these suggestions should come from an Ulsterman whose concern for his country had led to his joint authorship of a book, *Conflict and Christianity in Northern Ireland* (1976), which questioned how bright the prospects for peaceful coexistence in Northern Ireland could be while children were educated separately.

I thought his plans a second-best to the direct introduction of integrated education. I argued that if the government were to come out and say it was going for integrated education (not by compulsion but using means and methods to offer that option to parents), the move would be welcomed and accepted nationally and worldwide. At his request I put my views to him in writing. In a memorandum I wrote that Lagan College had at present 455 pupils (there would be 504 in September 1987), of whom 50 per cent were Protestant and 50 per cent Catholic (near enough). They spent 6.50 hours a day with each other for 190 days a year, that is, 1,235 hours every year. $1,235 \times 455 =$ 561,925 hours every year of interaction. There would be 31 teachers in September (equally divided between Catholic and Protestant). There were 387 prospective pupils on the waiting list already. Those all had mothers and fathers, brothers and sisters, uncles and aunts etcetera etcetera. The ripples extended out and beyond the college, and provided a power of community relations more effective than holiday schemes. It was constant, continuous interaction day in and day out that could bring about change in a big way, I argued. Community relations in a shared school like Lagan College would be available for the cost of the education of the children – in other words, at no extra cost. There was no substitute for integrated schooling, and it had been demonstrated time and again over the past fifteen years or so that a very significant number of parents in Northern Ireland supported it. Could we afford to set aside even in the meantime this obvious catalyst in favour of other alternatives which could not have the same reconciliatory effect on following generations of our children?

Two years later, through its Education Reform (Northern Ireland) Order, the government committed itself to support initiatives towards the development of planned integrated schools. It would provide 100 per cent funding on the condition that Education for Mutual Understanding and Cultural Heritage would become compulsory cross-curricular themes in the new common curriculum for all schools. It took a tough centrist of the calibre of Mawhinney, with a surprising open-mindedness and who was not easily deflected from his purpose, to overcome the resistance of a notoriously reactionary Department of Education.

The Education Reform (Northern Ireland) Order of 1989 was to impose a statutory duty upon the department to encourage and facilitate the development of integrated education. This was a victory. A sea-change had taken place which was to lead to the development of a 'third sector' in the Northern Ireland system of education. Moreover, Mawhinney's interest in Lagan College in particular and in integrated education in general was no astute political exercise in socioeducational engineering. It sprang from a genuinely held conviction.

In 1991, Dr Colin Irwin of the Department of Social Anthropology at Queen's University studied the friendship patterns of more than seven hundred pupils at Lagan College. (His findings have been widely published, the most recent of which is 'Social Conflict and Education Policy' in *Culture and Policy in Northern Ireland*, edited by Hastings Donnan and Graham McFarlane, 1997.) He invited the children to write down their thoughts and experiences. Clearly every boy and girl had been, to a greater or lesser degree, touched by the Troubles:

Protestant girl aged fifteen: 'Where I live it's all Protestants who are very bigoted and narrow minded. Before I came here I was one myself, I knew Catholics as Taigs, Fenians, Left Footers etc. I'd never met a Catholic before I sat beside one in class, they looked the same as me, they weren't like the kids made them out to be back home. Most of my best friends at school are Catholics and they're just like everyone else. I wish people where I lived would realise the same. Where I live there's a centre but with lots of shops and if you cross the road to the next street you're in an area where all Catholics live. So the shops are in the middle of the two religions. Who are as bad as each other, bigots. So any time a group of Protestants and Catholics are at the shops there's fights and people get badly hurt. But most of the time there's groups which wait about for fights. I wish they would feel as I do. If only they knew how normal they were. So most people can't go to the shops without getting a hiding.'

Catholic boy aged twelve: 'I live in Northern Ireland. Most of my life in the Belfast area. Some things are good about it but most are not very nice. I don't like the Troubles in Northern Ireland because it makes Belfast have a bad name. I really don't like all the killing that goes on because at times there was rocket launchers fired outside my house and machine gun fire. I don't like the Brits but I wouldn't want them killed. Before I went to this school I thought Protestants were scum but I don't think that now because my best friend is one. And he is not scum.'

Catholic girl aged fifteen: 'My first day at Lagan College was not what I expected it to be. . . . I remember thinking to myself why isn't everybody blessing themselves and then it dawned on me that Protestants don't bless themselves. I think a lot of Protestants were looking around thinking that the people blessing themselves looked like right idiots. Anyway, since then I've learnt that Protestants have a different ending to the Lord's Prayer, don't bless themselves and don't know what the Hail Mary is. In the five years I've been here I have been asked so many questions from Protestants like what's Communion and the Hail Mary. I have also asked people about their religion because I'm interested and want to know about what they do believe in and they are just as interested in my beliefs and views.'

Protestant boy aged thirteen: 'I am George I am a Protestant from a Protestant area. My best friend is Pat, he is a Catholic from a fairly Catholic area of Belfast. We met on our first day of school, he asked what religion I was, I told him. He told me he was a Catholic. I had never had a Catholic friend before. We are best friends now and we go into town on Saturdays but he is a bit scared to come to my house in case he gets beat up. But he is coming to my house for my birthday party. I have been to his house and I don't mind going his way. I have some other Catholic friends like Kevin and Brian.'

It has been the policy of Lagan College to have explained and argued out the intransigent beliefs and unacceptable politics, actions and attitudes of the 'others'. This practice was clearly vindicated on the Monday morning after the murder of corporals Howes and Wood to which I have already referred. That day the atmosphere was heavy with recrimination – some Catholic pupils asking how it was that the loyalist Michael Stone a few days previously had managed to get into Milltown cemetery and shoot Catholics, and some Protestant pupils asking how it is that so many Catholics are allowed to gather together at Catholic funerals. Classes were adjourned and children and staff gathered in the Assembly Hall. Free rein was given to individual views. The tense situation was defused. All went quietly back to the classroom to resume their places beside each other.

At the time of publication of this book there are 964 boys and girls on the roll (well on the way to the optimum of 1,200) and 72 teaching staff. Many former pupils have graduated from university, which they entered by means of the International Baccalauréat which the college uses in place of A levels. There are thirty-seven other integrated schools up and running throughout Northern Ireland now – altogether catering for the education of over 8,300 children.

There can be added to this a significant number of Catholic boys and girls on the rolls of Protestant grammar schools whose parents have sent them there preferring the mixed schooling experience for their children as well as choosing for them some of the finest schools anywhere – these schools, too, are helping to bridge the current divides. But educating Catholic and Protestant children together, fast becoming a widespread article of faith, cannot alone solve all the problems of the Northern Ireland community. What it can do is free children from suspicion, from the cynicism of despair and from the futile gloom imposed upon the community in the last three decades, and endeavour to ensure that the bitterness of these terrible times will not linger in their minds or be inherited by their children.

Northern Ireland politicians have largely ignored the plea for integrated education as a way forward towards that aim – if they ever addressed its desirability at all. Some may have paid lip service to it, but integrated education has not appeared prominently on the agenda of any Northern Ireland political party. It is regarded as irrelevant to basic political problems, something to think about some time in the future – but not just now. The attitude seems to be, first settle the tribal disputes and then look at the possibilities of integrated education helping to maintain peace if and when it comes. I believe politicians continue to ignore this vital issue at their peril. Integrated education is part of the 'peace process', and one can only hope that the education system at the end of the next decade will reflect a pluralistic society. Civilisation, after all, as Auden says, is to do with 'a unity which can be attained and a diversity which can be retained'.

Towards the end of 1988 I received a letter from Lord Ashby, one time vice-chancellor and chancellor of Queen's University, requesting information about Lagan College. He had been in contact with Deane Yates, deputy chairman of the New Era Schools' Trust in South Africa, to whom he had mentioned the work of the college. Deane Yates wrote to my principal, then Terence Flanagan (now headmaster of Rainey Endowed School, Magherafelt), whose wise and dedicated leadership did so much to build up Lagan College as a conspicuous school in the education system. In his letter Deane Yates wrote:

> We have been struck with the significant similarities between the philosophy of Lagan College and that of the New Era Schools' Trust and we believe that it would be beneficial to both our organisations if we were to share our experiences and learn from each other from face to face contact.... It might well be that we have a message which on its own merits might be proclaimed internationally.

In October 1989, Deane Yates came to Lagan College to discuss with us the prospective values of integrated education in Northern Ireland and the trust's interracial philosophy for South Africa. The board of directors of the college happily supported a visit by our principal to South Africa from 15 to 23 September 1990. He visited interracial schools in

Natal and Johannesburg, was interviewed by the South African Broadcasting Corporation, and attended a conference, entitled Schools of the Future, organised by the 'Institute for a Democratical Alternative in South Africa', where the keynote speech was given by the ANC director of education. Lagan College's contribution to the interracial debate in South Africa in the context of the schools there has not been insignificant – something good coming out of Northern Ireland for a change.

This anonymous letter from a soldier who had served in Northern Ireland was received in Lagan College following the Shankill Road bombing in October 1993 in which ten people were killed:

LETTER FROM A WELL-WISHER

. . . I have just read about your school in the *Express* newspaper, included in the article about the Shankill killings. Could I offer you some outside words of encouragement for the future in what your school is doing? I am a retired soldier still coming to terms with some of the horror I saw on the streets of Belfast where I served out two years of my life as a front line soldier. I am in fact lying in a Catholic hospital run by nuns, recovering from an operation to repair damage to my spine which originated in a bomb blast near the Markets in 1979.

Putting all of the pain to one side, I must tell you that my strongest memories of Northern Ireland are not of violence but of a wonderful people, rich in giving, full of love, people who from both sides took us in, fed us, bathed our wounds, people who often kept us smiling in the face of death.

Some of these people paid for our friendship with their lives, being killed over a cup of tea. I will never forget the real heroes of Ulster, the people who follow Christ's basic teaching: 'Love thy neighbour.' As I left Ulster for the last time I thought what a waste of a people, of Ireland, what a waste of a nation. Perhaps the children will change the future. Well, the IRA bomber on Saturday was only a child when I left and look what he did! It brought all the old feelings back. Faces of people long since dead. But upon reading about yours and other integrated schools, it filled me with joy to think maybe I was right. The future does lie with the children. This is the first time I have ever put my feelings about Ireland on paper. I hope they give you some support.

God's blessings on you all.

K.H.

26 October 1993

The chaos of the past three decades has shown that the men of violence, and the bigots in Northern Ireland society have cared little for what happens to their children – children divided deeply along denominational and cultural lines, which has left at least two generations of them unlikely to be qualified to promote future harmony. The quickest and most vicious way of destroying a child is to teach it to hate – hate that will fester until the day it dies.

For some time to come, children will continue to throw stones at each other over the 'peacelines' in Belfast because they are either Protestant or Catholic. Those who would divide can only succeed if they can pass their hatred on. Our children have been asked to carry that baggage of fear and hatred into an increasingly cynical and predatory world.

Those of us involved in establishing integrated schools believe that, where integration operates from the board of governors down through the staff and the children, integrated schools will lead to improved community relations through increased understanding and tolerance, recognising and accommodating diversity. Preserving diversity while moving children into a new era of democracy and pluralism is the task ahead.

Our children will decide what the future is to be, for did not Christ once stand a child in front of the crowd and say, in effect, 'This is your future'?

ON REFLECTION

THE NECESSARY AND INEVITABLE SOCIAL REFORMS of the sixties, which evoked so much resentment and which were so vigorously resisted by an ungenerous Unionist establishment, are long since in place. Over the past thirty years a fairer and more just society has been steadily growing, under the light of national and international scrutiny and publicity which has badly damaged unionism.

But the fairer deployment of material well-being amongst the people will not in itself bring peace. This has to come from hearts and minds. Alas, in Northern Ireland polarisation is running deeper than ever before. Doctrinaire loyalism, which refuses to recognise that every right has a corresponding duty, still upholds old shibboleths such as 'not an inch' long past their sell-by date, to the embarrassment of mainstream unionism. Why else did grassroots unionists stay at home at the May 1997 local elections if not because politicians were saying nothing new or hopeful, and because frustration with the politicians made these unionists feel alienated from the political process? On the other side, nationalists continue to find themselves placed between aspiration and hope, manipulated by clever Sinn Féin politicians enjoying increasing successes at the polls.

One cannot help but admire the audacity of their beguiling argument that the proper place for unionists with their unique identity is within a united Ireland. In common with at least 40 per cent of Northern Ireland citizens I have always regarded myself as Irish – not English – but with a tradition of Britishness. There is no good reason why such a sizeable grouping should feel apologetic about wishing to remain part of one of the most stable and enviable countries in the world, with its constitutional monarchy one of its strengths. A.T.Q. Stewart has expressed a similar opinion (*Belfast Telegraph*, 29 November 1994):

> The only guarantee of our rights lies in Northern Ireland remaining part of the UK.
> With all its faults, which at least are frequently and copiously revealed, it is the most dependable of the western democracies, and essentially the fairest.

The Stormont establishment, with its background of privilege and patronage and its unwillingness to come to terms with the problem of democratic participation, held within itself the seeds of its own destruction. A reconstructed Stormont would now be inconceivable. The survival of Northern Ireland within the United Kingdom is accepted by a treaty between Westminster and Dublin as depending on the consent of the majority of Northern Ireland's people. No doubt the concept of consent will cause trouble. It is an imponderable around which much controversy and attempted fudging by republicans will take place. But it has at last become clear that republicans accept the reality that a united Ireland cannot and never will be achieved through force of arms. Irish unity, if it ever comes, is a long way off. Instead I believe that the wheel will turn full circle and the 1973 Sunningdale powersharing experiment will be reintroduced in one form or another, replacing direct rule from Westminster. This will permit true democracy to work, which will bring the administration of Northern Ireland closer to the people; and it will also embrace close formal links with the Irish Republic. This return to local democracy can only be achieved by courageous Unionist politicians who will dare to take risks, who will refuse to walk away from the unpleasant necessity of speaking to the enemy, who will be prepared to negotiate but always wary of the republicans edging their way by stealth towards a united Ireland. It is a sign of great hope that recent polls show the majority of unionists in favour of inclusive talks with nationalists and republicans.

As for the brutal terrorist whose way of life is to kill and maim, and those who threaten to continue to wade through slaughter for as long as it takes to 'free' Ireland, he or she must be outlawed and offered no hiding place. This can only happen when those who delude themselves in believing that the terrorists are heroes, possessing the purest revolutionary virtues, cry 'Enough!' and disown them.

There is a long way to go in the search for peace, stability and reconciliation. As Shelley tells us in *Prometheus Unbound*, we must continue

> . . . to hope till Hope creates
> From its own wreck the thing it contemplates.

INDEX